MARCUS

MYSTERIOUS

WESSON

WEB

of DECEPTION

By Julia Dudley Najieb

Many blessing.
Sincerely,
Julia Dudley Najieb

An Ann Marie Production
United States

An Ann Marie Production

Research Team
Johnny Sharp
Lennice Najieb
Ramona Washington
Julia Dudley Najieb

Graphic Designer: Ernst Shadday
Illustrator: Nadi Spencer
Page & Layout Design: Dick Tris

Publisher: Ann Marie Production
Research Interviewer: Lennice Najieb
Interview Transcriber: Tanya Ghanam

Photography Consultant: Ken McCoy
All Photos by Ken McCoy:
Wesson motor home bus photo
Community reaction photo
Chaplains carrying the coffin photo
Two coffins photo
Fresno Police Chief Jerry Dyer photo

Proof Reading Editing Team:
Tanya Ghanam
Niama Muhammad
Cary Catalano
Ramona Cheek
Ramona "Ms. Diva" Washington
Lujuanja Bull
Chris Finley, Sr.
Lennice Najieb
Clark Sumner
Johnny Sharp

All Photos by Johnny Sharp:
Two 761 Hammond Ave. front house photos
Two 761 Hammond Ave. backyard house photos

Wesson Extended Family Web Chart
Created by Chris Finley, Sr., Carmella Johnson and Dick Tristao

Public Relations & Marketing Consultant: Cary Catalano
Legal Consultant: Sean Onderick

Marcus Wesson: *Mysterious Web of Deception*
© 2005 Julia Dudley Najieb & Ann Marie Production

ISBN: 0-9763860-8-9

An **Ann Marie Production**
4974 N. Cedar PBM 139
Fresno, CA 93726-1063
For more information about our products:
1-800-971-6498
www.annmarieproduction.com

Dedicated to those still searching for something more than religion, more than themselves, in hopes to find peace.

Contents

Acknowledgements

Throughout this project, there were a number of difficult tasks to overcome; however, I am very appreciative of having good friends and a loving family that helped us through the tough moments. I thank my friend Maureen for her guidance to move forward with this project, even when we weren't sure where to begin.

I certainly thank my friend Johnny Sharp who after hearing about the project took off full-force with ideas, research, interviews and strategies to get a big jump on this case; things would not have moved forward as fast if it wasn't for his diligence.

What would we have done without my good friend and business partner Ramona "Ms. Diva" Washington, paving the way for the publicity, help and encouragement throughout the tedious process? Her wonderful positive attitude kept things afloat, even during the most difficult times.

I thank my brother Greg for being supportive and for getting us the appropriate legal assistance and advice necessary and Sean for his consulting that should have cost us an arm and leg.

I would definitely like to pay my respects to Lujuana for taking the time out of her very busy schedule to give the necessary constructive criticism and editing needed to make this book a success.

Juanita, we appreciate your advice and assistance in the initial stages of this project; we were able to find a clearer direction in our research and book format.

Without the humor of Joe, Tanya and Clark, life would have been too serious and not as much fun throughout this project. I thank Tanya for her patience, understanding, and God-light that was inspiring; I also appreciated her wonderful editing skills and suggestions to help make this book a success.

I also thank my neighbors and friends Joann, Jesse, Bryan, and Dora for always being supportive on all projects great and small; it's nice to have wonderful, caring neighbors.

Chris Finley, Sr., your intellect and knowledge has always amazed me; thank goodness you are a friend and have always been there.

Cary Catalano, what can I say, a man of his word and a friend who stuck with us through the thick and thin of this project.

I certainly can't forget my friend and colleague Ms. Cheek for her positive support; she was a soundboard for all of my woes and whimpers. Also, I thank my first period English II students—2004-2005 school year—I enjoyed teaching and learned a lot from our current-event class discussions; it was a joy and a pleasure to start the day off with this group of bright students everyday. Also Coaches Johnson and Berkey, you have always been very supportive in all projects and stepped up in my absence and I am sincerely grateful for your compassion, friendship and understanding. The staff, administration and friends at Fresno High are always supportive and encouraging; I appreciate it.

I thank my cousins, family members and best friends for never giving up on me and keeping me strong through all projects: Aunt Chris, Sherri, Mike, Anne, Michael Dudley, Rosemary Dudley, Teresa McKinney, Dr. Terry Miller and children Kamau, Jabari, and Jameelah.

Thank you Ms. Oprah Winfrey for reminding me there are no limits, no matter the skin tone.

Husband, Lennice, without you, I know things would not have excelled as they did; you are a precious gem, a talented resource, I don't know how I could ever repay you but with love and the utmost respect.

I thank New Thought for keeping me grounded in God's love.

I thank my mother and father for teaching me to strive against all odds; even in the face of adversity, stand tall and smile victory

"Knowledge is in the end based on acknowledgement."

~ Ludwig Wittgenstein

Foreword

Role Models for Truth
Presenting Another Perspective

Marcus Wesson: Mysterious Web of Deception, written and published by Julia Dudley Najieb and Ramona Washington a.k.a. Ms. Diva, is an untold story about the shocking and frightening Wesson mass murders. They have reached into the psyche and lives of the victims to reveal a perspective that goes far beyond the news accounts of this tragedy. The book covers the story from a viewpoint that only compelled black women could chronicle. It is paramount that the readers of this account have an understanding of who these black women are and why they elected to invest their talents and precious time to conduct the required research and develop a trusting relationship with the often ignored and misunderstood remaining family members who hold some of the keys to understanding the case.

Why would two talented, beautiful and successful women want to write about such a heinous incident that is addressed in the book? Julia Dudley Najieb is a high school English teacher, track & field coach, author/publisher, wife and mother. Ms. Diva is a celebrity hair stylist, business owner, singer/actress, publisher and mother. In short, both women are blessed with a host of creative talents and are deeply involved in their community. It would seem they would be too busy and too satisfied with their comfortable lifestyles to even give the situation more than a sympathetic glance. Julia and Miss Diva are guided by their values, integrity, love and compassion, and have created this book out of a sense of obligation to present little known facts about a very complex situation. They took on the task simply because they cared about the lives of the people affected by this tragedy.

These women are strong examples of people who are never too busy to be concerned about the condition and safety of other women and children. They have tackled this tragedy to help women understand their self-worth and to identify characteristics in a relationship that imprison the body, mind and spirit. Delving into this incident has the power to release those secrets that so many women harbor that can lead to impotent lives for themselves and their families.

While reading this book, pray for the authors, the living Wesson victims trapped in a painful existence and those women, children and families who are in unhealthy relationships. Pray that this book will give them the strength and resources to recover and move into a life full of the joy that the Creator has willed for us all. Thanks to the authors for not being satisfied with their level of comfort, but using their time and talents to help others. By creating this book, these women have taken this very uncomfortable and unimaginable situation and shown the strong empathetic nature of Black women.

Julia and Ms. Diva are simply Role Models for Truth presenting another perspective.

Lafayette Jones
February 2005

Lafayette Jones is a nationally syndicated columnist and publisher.

Introduction

Sudden rolling thunder; that's what it is like when a person hears about a horrific mass murder happening right in his or her own backyard … For me it was a different experience: it was a very late night March 12, 2004 when I came home from a local track meet; I coach track & field at an inner-city high school in Fresno. That day was unusual: Mercury was retrograde, and all running and jumping events were running incredibly behind because the night lights would not come on the track; I was deliriously exhausted. I don't think I got home until after 10 o'clock that night. I remember the bed being the most euphoric, comfortable place for me to lay my tired, aching bones. I switched on the television to a special report that continually flashed across the screen. Between my intermittent slumber, I could barely grasped what was happening. I think I dreamed about Police Chief Jerry Dyer several times, not realizing it was him speaking throughout the night about this infamous case. It was also Dyer's words that woke me around 11 PM from my drowsiness.

Then the panic hit me; for some reason I pictured a white man killing people in the neighborhood. At that time, my husband was working out of town so I was really concerned. I slowly began to prop myself up and listen to the newscast. There still was not a clear picture of who this so-called mass murderer was, readily killing people in the neighborhood, and I wondered, "Was he close by?" Suddenly, I realized it was much deeper than that; family members were dead. In my mind, "Oh, great, some crazy white boy done lost his job and his mind."

Boy was I wrong: the description slowly came in spurts of a man with dreadlocks. For a split second I thought perhaps it was a white man with dreadlocks who married a black woman, they must have been mistaken; maybe he just didn't comb his hair and it was all matted up and looked that way—I had seen that before.

More and more information continued to flow: Children.

Youngest to oldest. Seven dead. "We finally found the last two young bodies," said Chief Dyer... "It's nine." And it was a black man proclaimed as the killer. Not only that, it was soon discovered that he was also the father of his daughter's children that were found dead that evening—Incest!

My first question was, "How did this happen?" My next set of questions were: "Why here in Fresno? What happened to this man? Where did life stop him? Why the incestual relations?"

Immediately I began my search for more information on the case as it slowly filtered the media and newsstands. This was much bigger than I thought, even down to the arrangements of the body and how it all occurred. I talked to a few of my old-time friends and business associates about the case. We discussed the whys', the hows' and the whos' of the matter, hoping to find one defined answer.

Monday morning, March 15th, I went into my classroom ready to teach, but questioning eyes were not focused on high school English that day; they were focused on the horrifics of what we now knew as the Wesson murders. The murder scene was less than one mile away from the high school; I felt it was time to talk about fears and help dispel them.

Students wanted to know why and how things transpired. We discussed *The Fresno Bee* newspaper article in class, read it together aloud, and went over the main issues. The one point I told them to remember from all of this was for them to always investigate situations for themselves; always look at the full scope of a picture. "Don't believe everything you hear; there's always three sides to a story," I told them.

There was one student who approached, bringing me to the side after class and informing of a friend's cousin who was related to the 17 year-old Wesson daughter who died. The student went on to explain the eccentricities of the family, their extreme religious practices, the cultist behavior, and the usual teenager rebellions occurring within the family structure that assisted in this family's tragic memory of a real live Hamlet nightmare. It was then that I began to question what was fact and what was fiction.

I placed my mind into the research mode to find out the truth and to find out who the victims really were. In my formulated opinion, the mothers that were still alive in the Wesson family were truly victims as well, but of another crime. This crime involved manipulation of the heart and soul, and words... Words are so powerful; they can make a man weep, feel happy and build enough anger to kill.

What's more powerful than words themselves?

Religious words; they can hold men at ease to a conscience of despair if they have behaved wrongly or betrayed their faith in any way. Such doctrines hold men at peace or in fear.

For this family, religion was the pillar of hope and despair.

The more I began to research this case, the stranger it seemed; I met the Wesson family members who were portrayed very differently in the media and by peering neighbors who said they knew this family. I retrieved insights from law enforcement about the calm, cool collective behavior of Marcus Wesson; for a big-time mass murderer, I wondered if such behavior was out of character. Soon my eyes were open to the true killer of these children, and this is where the story of ironic twists and sharp turns begins.

"A wise man will hear, and will increase learning; and a man of understanding shall attain unto wise counsels..."
~Old Testament Book of Proverbs, 1:5; *The Bible*
(King James Version)

Alpha

The Beginning of Wisdom

In most William Shakespearean tragedies, there is a mass death of several related characters to remind us of the foolishness of man's ego when he selfishly allows his emotions to run his thoughts, decision and beliefs. Through such characters as Hamlet, portrayed as the avenging delusional son, we notice the human psyche that reasons and justifies societal wrongs such as murder; "I was betrayed by the infidelities of my own mother who married my uncle—my father's brother—right after my father's suspicious death." These were good reasons for Hamlet to kill them all, at least in his mind.

Hamlet's ego stepped in to tell him everything he was doing was right and for a good purpose; the integrity of his family values, history and name under his father's reign. His ego, represented by the soul of his unrest, revengeful father, convinced him that the plotting and planning of each murder he would pursue was for a better cause. Reasoning became a coping mechanism for irrational acts.

Although the portrayal of unrest souls depicting hurt egos was common in such Elizabethan literature, no one would ever think to bring such hysterics into today's reality. However it is a thought to address for a murder unbelievable: The Wesson family murders portrayed a true tragedy of such unrest, emotional hysterics and betrayal layered with incest—an ego unimaginable.

No one ever knows what to believe when a crime of nine deaths at once has been committed within one family; it almost seems surreal. The only assured fact in such a case is that a gun and a gunman are at fault to something much more.

As a research team, we pondered these questions that would only evoke silent answers:
Why did this happen?
Why all of the children?
Who really did this?
What were the premises behind this shooting?
Why didn't the victims try to escape?
Who is the Wesson family and where are they from?
Who is Marcus Wesson?

Why would a black man murder his own family?

This case was so grim that every resource we turned to seemed to lead to a dead end. It was inevitable that the district attorney's office had to keep its mouth shut. At one point the media was our best source to clues and answers; although, there were still many gaps that needed to be filled. We attempted to send notes through people and attorneys who knew the family to let them know we were an earnest group of researchers trying to create a fair story and synopsis: the problem was people had already harbored this idea, taking advantage of the family's situation for the worst. This only distanced the Wesson family more from any direct media contact or questions from observers, researchers or others seeking gain for pain. Shunned by the community, and misinterpreted by the media, cautioned the recluse family to not trust a soul.

However, on a cliché—a wing and a prayer—things began to come together. In time clues began to make sense, witnesses began to talk to us and the immediate Wesson family members of this tragedy slowly began to chat with us as well.

As a result of blessings, we are able to clear up some inconsistent facts spread through the media and explain some of the Wesson family phenomena misunderstood by most of the public, who could never fathom such a massacre.

As the trial commences in early spring, many stories will circulate via the television media of this unique family, the bizarre murders, and the inimitable defendant, Marcus Wesson. What we simply hope to do is make the reader more aware of facts, circumstances, family values and backgrounds so that he or she may decide for him or herself who is culpable. We wish to bring the reader insight to the main mother, Elizabeth, and her children who bore children with Marcus—her husband—not for judgment of who's wrong or right, but for clarity and acknowledgment of information. We hope readers are then able to make up their own minds.

As the lengthy trial unfolds, we will continue to write and reveal facts as we know them. However, for the moment, may we intrigue readers with the preliminaries ...

Marcus Wesson: Mysterious Web of Deception entails the true accounts of one of the largest and most unusual mass murders to ever plague the San Joaquin Valley.

On March 12, 2004, chaos broke the peace of the close-knit community at 761 Hammond Ave., Fresno, Ca. The bloodied, accused Marcus Wesson surrendered himself at gunpoint to Fresno police officers and the SWAT team. His cooperative and emotionless demeanor was disturbing to all who watched the plot unfold. Inside the house was a horrid crime scene, where a heap of nine bodies lay intertwined in a bedroom corner: nine victims of a bizarre shooting, each shot in the eye. All of the deceased victims were offspring of Marcus Wesson; no signs of struggle from any of them were apparent before their murders. Several coffins were found at the murder scene causing some to believe the homicides were premeditated.

Practicing incestual relations with his daughters and nieces, according to DNA evidence, Marcus fathered all of the deceased victims, which would also question who the killer really was; forensic evidence and gunpowder residue testing would show that he was not the shooter of the gun. Yet there were other puzzle pieces that seem to fit; the cultish activities of the inter-reliant family deeply involved in their own-made religion, headed by Marcus, himself.

Very few knew this recluse, nomadic family who lived up and down the California coasts, valleys and mountains. Resourceful and thrifty, the Wesson family kept silent under the radar, birthing child after child, without a single soul knowing or reporting the long-term oddities and eccentricities of their habits and life style. There were no school, birth, or hospital records of any of the victims or Wesson children who survived.

Twisted with a paradox of those who knew this generous, kind family, interviews with their former friends and immediate family members ironically distance the murder scene from their modest and humble countenance, along with their genuinely sincere disposition; keeping the reader intensely mystified by the acts of kindness, mortified by the sexual and finale acts of murder.

Intriguing preliminary testimony unfolds the mass plot, identifying the deceased Wesson children and the living ones with clarity and understanding. The lewd sex acts Mr. Wesson had with his daughters and nieces are specifically detailed; formidable to any outsider who is usually able to stomach descriptions and scenes of healthy intercourse with one partner. This book goes beyond the extremes and norms of the love and affection a father would have for his children; so far beyond that adults, age 18 or under, should be advised of the intense sexual content that would not be appropriate otherwise.

Read the calculations and interpretations of the Wesson family dynamics and values provided by Dr. Eric Hickey, a notable criminology professor and celebrated author of his recent book, *Serial Murderers and Their Victims*.

Become enlightened by Fresno renowned criminal defense attorney Ernest Kinney and other expert commentaries of the upcoming trial and possible judgments Marcus Wesson faces.

Join us as we unravel the hidden mysteries of the Wesson family that are finally explored and resolved as the reader weaves through the revelations of the book, creating a web of understanding.

"Time will explain it all. He is a talker, and needs no questioning before he speaks."
~Aeolus. Frg.38.

WESSON EXTENDED FAMILY WEB

The nine victims were fathered by Marcus Wesson with six women, two of whom were his daughters, three were his nieces.

"...in much wisdom is much grief: and he that increaseth knowledge increaseth sorrow."
~Old Testament Book of Ecclesiastes, 1:18;
The Bible

Revelation 1

The Tragedy that Revealed the Hidden Culmination

761 Hammond, a house on a corner of a temperate highway and quiet neighborhood street. Children play outside in their yards, an old man strolls down the paved sidewalk with his walking cane. The one-story houses carry their own personalities by way of design and a little human touch. Some lawns are well kept with edging flowerbeds happily sprouting in fresh dirt. Other lawns are a little frumpy but not hurtful to the eye that scans the neighborhood to find that this is just one ordinary block, in an ordinary Californian neighborhood at peace.

Except the corner house, 761 Hammond Ave., hides in shadows behind huge evergreens that protect its nature and inhabitants. A light gray complexioned exterior gives the house its meekness; one would not dare to complain of this office house not being kept up as flowers beds decorate the side of the house. The concrete, windy walkway, shaded by trees, brings one to the office-house door where one can see in the window the common sign of most business offices out to lunch that says, "We'll be back at 1:45." However these odd things would not outrageously disturb the neighbors for several months.

Zoned as a commercial residence, formerly a credit union for the Southern Pacific Railroad, the Wesson family of almost 15 people lived within its walls and adapted to the one-story, three bedroom pride and joy; they had lived there for just eight months before the events would unfold. A bystander may ask, "How did they do it, how did that many people live happily in one tiny corner office space called home?" According to the youngest son Serafino, they were always well taken care of, no matter their circumstance, and they were a close-knit family that stuck together.

A family closed off to the world opened its window to its soul when murder disrupted the status quo and way of life on 761 Hammond Ave. Nine murders of sons, daughters and grandchildren revealed the covered truths of wrongs concealed; a mysterious web of deception larger than life itself—all of the deceased children were fathered by Marcus Wesson.

It would be only Marcus who would walk out of a southeast bedroom of the house alive that day—March 12, 2004; the other nine bloody victims he stacked in the corner of the room, youngest to oldest, intertwining the body parts with clothing strips and blankets.

A scene massed in blood and coffins of antique wood would be described by Police Chief Jerry Dyer to be one of the worst cases in his 25 years in the Fresno Police Department that he had ever experienced; never anything of this nature in Fresno's crime history. Some officers cried on site as they tried to unmask one of the worst mass murders in Fresno; they would later be given paid administrative leave and time with a psychologist to grasp the unimaginable of what they saw: the piled bodies of children—all offspring of Marcus Wesson—ranging from age 13 months to 25 years of age. The nine victims were identified: Sebhrenah April Wesson, 25, female (mother—Elizabeth Wesson); Elizabeth Breahi Kina Wesson, 17, female (mother—Elizabeth Wesson); Illabella Carrie Wesson, 8, female (mother—Kiani Wesson); Ethan St. Laurent Wesson, 4, male (mother Rosie Solorio); Sedonia Vadra Wesson, 1 1/2, female (mother Rosie Solorio); Marshey St. Christopher Wesson, 1 1/2, male (mother—Sebhrenah Wesson); Jeva St. Vladensvspry Wesson, 1, male (mother—Kiani Wesson); Aviv Dominique Wesson, female (mother—Ruby Sanchez) and Johnathan St. Charles Wesson, male (mother –Sofina Solorio), both 7 years old. All of the children were shot in the right eye at close range; except for Sebhrenah's son Marshey, he was shot in the left eye.

Cause of death was determined to be immediate "perforation of brain" caused by a gunshot wound to the face; Illabella died of a "contusion of the brain" after being shot in the face. There were no signs of struggle, abuse or mutilation among any of the victims.

The 57 year-old Marcus Wesson was initially charged with nine counts of murder in the first degree in violation of Penal Code Section 187 and originally 13 sex counts, including rape and molestation of girls younger than 14. His bail amount was set at $9,270,000 for all nine counts.

Marcus pleaded not guilty to all charges; if convicted, he could face the death penalty.

The prosecution wanted to find a way to link the sex allegations with the nine counts of murder; 33 more sexual counts were added by the prosecution at the preliminary hearing April 8, 2004. Judge R.L. Putnam had been assigned to the preliminary hearing.

In an arraignment, Judge Brant Bramer told Wesson that an investigation revealed that he didn't have enough money to hire the lawyer he had chosen, David Mugridge. Bramer then appointed public defender Peter Jones to take the case.

Two previous attempts to arraign Wesson had to be postponed when he refused to accept a public defender.

Problems before the Murders

A dispute of child custody brought this family into the eyesight of the outside world. Two nieces of Marcus and Elizabeth Wesson, Sofina Solorio (also recognized as Sofia) and Ruby Garcia-Sanchez, went to the home earlier that day to retrieve their children. From a preliminary hearing, April 8th to April 12, 2004, under the Honorable Judge Lawrence Jones in the Fresno Superior Court, police and detective testimonies help unravel the mystery behind the massacre.

According to the testimony of detective Michele Ochoa who spoke to Sofia four days after the murders, in 2003, Sofia—who had run away from the Wesson home and was forbidden to see the family or visit the children, including her own child—was slowly allowed back into the Wesson family due to the Wessons need for rent, money and food. They would call her while she was in San Jose, Ca. working and Marcus, Kiani and Rosie would travel to her to pick up money for their housing and food. This allowed Sofia to come back around the family; she would also bring clothing, food and medicine. What alarmed Sofia once coming back around the family was the three new babies: Kiani's, Rosie's and Sebrhenah's. This was shocking to Sofia because she was told by Sebhrenah that she never wanted a child and wanted to leave the residence and get married. None of the girls were working, there was no income and the children were not being educated. According to Sofia, there was normal Bible study in the mornings and afternoon and yet the scene she saw was nothing of the sort; children were running around while other family members were sitting around watching TV. Her concerns became for the children whom she noticed looked very skinny and sickly where Marcus was overweight. Even the girls, she said, looked very thin. Then Sofia was told by Kiani that Jeva had been so sickly he almost died. In confronting Marcus, Sofia told him she was concerned about him continuing to have children with his own children due to deformities and society's or the world's view of such unacceptable behavior. She feared that they would soon find out about his horrible family secret; thus, she felt the situation was jeopardizing her own son, fearing that he was in danger. According to Sofia, Marcus told her that the girls agreed to it and they were going to raise the children, not get married, and stay with him.

Then several weeks prior to the March 12th incident there was a significant agreement made: Ochoa said that Marcus asked Sofia to claim Johnathan on her taxes so that he could get the money for Johnathan. Sofia would agree with this only on the premise that she would be allowed to get her son back. This was her hope, to have physical custody of her son; to this, Marcus agreed. However, the entanglement began when the other daughter Gypsy used Jonathan on her taxes as a dependent. This, of course, broke the agreement. This would later spawn a new argument to get the children because there was no deal or money as an exchange. Sofia, knowing this, went to a plan B.

Later on, she went to her sister Ruby's house where they all were planning on meeting with a large support personnel—support staff of family members and relatives—so they could go to Marcus' house and get their children; Ruby also had a young daughter in the hands of Marcus that she wanted to retrieve. This idea was suggested by a counselor who felt that Marcus would give them their children through intimidation. Also, the ladies felt they needed the numbers due to their fear of him and of what they thought might happen. So they wanted to bring as many people as humanly possible, they had at least 15 people or more that went over with them to the Hammond house that day. One of those members included in the family support was their other younger sister Brandy Sanchez, who had claims of also being sexually victimized by Marcus like Sofia and Ruby; she was the first to run away from the Wesson home at age 17. Their main goal was to go to the house and retrieve Jonhathan and Aviv and possibly the girls, Kiani and Rosie, whom they refer to as their sisters, (Rosie is their blood sister).

The Afternoon of March 12th

In a present tense fashion, here is how the events unfolded:
Sofia is the first to arrive at the Hammond house that day. She first approaches Rosie and Elizabeth Jr.; Rosie tells her that mom, referring to the main wife of Marcus, Elizabeth isn't home. Sofia continues to walk into the residence where soon after her Uncle Michael and brother, Danny, arrive, which alarms Rosie who at this point wants to know what is going on, what was everyone doing at their house. Sofia continues to enter the household and witnesses her son from the living room in a glass bedroom. As soon as she sees him, she grabs him and begins to exit the bedroom with Jonathan. However, Rosie, her sister, then screams out, "No!" She grabs Johnathan's arms and puts them around her waist and backs herself up against the living room wall. Rosie then slowly makes her way down the hallway towards the last bedroom—the southeast bedroom. Sofia then rushes to the southeast bedroom to retrieve Johnathan again; however, Rosie continues to hold him behind her back while all of the sisters and cousins—who were like sisters—begin to argue. Things become very chaotic and out of control. As Sofia pushes her

way through people to get to the back room, she notices her cousin Elizabeth, Jr. putting other children as well into the room with the others that were already there, Marshey and Rosie's infant female Sedonia. She also notices her sister Ruby's child, Aviv, brought into the room by her cousin as well.

Meanwhile, Marcus is standing at the front door. While inside the room, Elizabeth, Jr. is yelling at the children to shut up and just sit there, as the girls are screaming at Sofia. The babies are all calm but scared. Sofia is eventually pushed out by Rosie, as a fight ensues, while Kiani, who is positioned outside the bedroom in the hallway, is pulling her out with force. Then the bedroom door closes; all of the children are in the room, including the oldest original Wesson daughter, Sebhrenah. Kiani rushes for a cell phone to call her mother Elizabeth, while Rosie is headed to the house phone. Unable to get her son, Sofia walks into the living room where she has a discussion with Marcus who wants them to all sit down and talk and try to work things out. However the panic begins as Sofia sees Rosie rush to the back room where the children and Sebhrenah are being held. She immediately runs to the southeast bedroom and tries to physically force the door open. She gets her body halfway through where she can now see Rosie piling up clothes and furniture. She then looks down to see Sebhrenah in a portion of the room, digging in her leather bag; the same leather bag that Marcus keeps his firearms. Unable to keep the door open with her bodily force, she is eventually closed out of the room. Marcus continues to urge that he and the girls talk about the situation, giving Sofia hope that she could have Johnathan. Finally, the three of them talk. Strangely Sofia notices Rosie and Kiani whispering in their dad, Marcus's ear, as she hears, "Dad, should we?" And Marcus replies to them no. Marcus then reaches in his pocket, pulls out a small pouch that has a key and some other dangling items and hands this over to Rosie. Shortly after, Serafino barges into the house angrily due to the commotion and chaos going on in front of the house. Kiani communicates to Serafino about Sofia wanting to take her child, as she continues to walk down the hallway of the southeast bedroom. Sofia eventually loses sight of both girls while Serafino is upset and out of anger makes a threat to Sofia's brother, Marco, that he was going to snap his neck.

Meanwhile, the older sister Sebhrenah is peeking out of the bedroom window and telling Sofia's sister Ruby, "all you mother fuckers get out of here!"

It is after Serafino's comment and the commotion going on that Sofia finally feels enough is enough; she wants to get the police involved and does. A relative from her support group calls the dispatch. Frank Nelson, a uniformed police officer arrives to 761 West Hammond at about 2:35 PM because of a child custody dispute. Nelson, an officer for 18 ½ years, views the situation as a routine domestic dispute. Apparently a neighbor had also called earlier about the disturbances at the house and possible gunshot noises. Another officer, Martinez also arrives at the same time as Nelson. They come onto the scene to where at least a 10 or more people are congregated in the front of the house, the supporters of Ruby and Sofia.

Meanwhile, Sofia exits the house and the officers both park their cars east of the location, walk towards a silver vehicle in front of the residence, and make contact with the two females, Sofia Solorio and Ruby Sanchez, the reporting parties who had no luck with the family in getting their children. Sofia tells the officer that she wants her child back.

Through the discovery of Officer Nelson's preliminary hearing testimony April 8, 2004, more things become clarified about the happenings on Hammond Avenue...

Officer Nelson tells Ruby and Sofia to wait while he makes contact with the family; the front door of the home is open. In the doorway stands a black male, Marcus Wesson. Officer Nelson can see Kiani and Rosie further in the house through the doorway. When questioned about who he is, Marcus tells the officer he is a friend of the family and that he stays there off and on as a guest. Officer Nelson explains to Marcus that he is there about a child custody dispute and that Sofia and Ruby have come to get their kids. Nelson asks to enter the house and Marcus tells him he cannot. Ruby and Sofia are about 20 feet behind both officers.

According to Officer Nelson, Sofia is lured back into the house by Kiani and Rosie who insist on talking about the situation and working it out, Ruby refuses. Meanwhile, Nelson continues to talk to Marcus in the doorway, questioning if he has court papers on the children explaining the guardianship. Marcus tells him that the kids were given to him eight years ago and that it was a verbal agreement. Earlier Ruby and Sofia showed Nelson a birth certificate, signifying they are the parents of the children in question. Marcus tells Nelson that he is going to let the nieces take the kids, but he needs a little more time to talk; he did not like the use of force.

Nelson informs him that since there is no legal court documentation of guardianship, then the mothers have a right to come and get their children. If necessary, Nelson tells him he would have to get the CPS involved. (CPS would be allowed to enter the house without a warrant before the police could.) Marcus remains calm, claiming he just wants to talk. Nelson asks Ruby and Sofia again if they want to talk; Ruby refuses, Sofia decides to talk one more time.

A few minutes later, Sergeant Jackson approaches the front door; Nelson gives him a briefing on the situation. Because of a noise made at one of the corners of the house, the sergeant asks Officer Martinez to go to the location. He then asks Nelson to do a records check on all the parties involved; Nelson goes back to his vehicle to do this. He then goes back to the sergeant who is still standing at the doorway, (Marcus initially agrees to let the sergeant enter but then changes his mind, giving the excuse that he doesn't think the girls want him in the house). Sofia and Ruby are then back at the doorway where Kiani and Rosie are still pleading with the distraught mothers to come in so that they can talk. Marcus stays calm the whole time and eventually asks the mothers to tell the truth. One of the mothers responds that if he wants them to, they will tell the truth about the abuse. Sofia enters the house one more time to talk to the Rosie and Kiani, according to Officer Nelson, but then at one point, she gets tired of talking and doesn't enter the house anymore. Sofia then tells the Officer Nelson that she is going to leave with her child or CPS will. *(Sister Brandy would later account in her testimony that she interpreted the officer telling Marcus, Rosie and Kiani that there would be three arrests because they were refusing to give up the children, and they were refusing to let the officer step inside of the house; CPS would be on there way without fail—this is what spun the deadly plan of death into action, according to Brandy. She also recalled Kiani and Ruby yelling to Sofia, "Obey your master," master referring to Marcus; a term Marcus often taught to the girls so that they would refer to him as the Lord.)*

By this time, Sofia is out of the house again when her aunt Elizabeth arrives to the scene with her mother, Rosemary, who is driving the car erratically to get to the Hammond house. Her own mother angrily rushes out of the car, causing a lot of commotion with everybody, according to Ruby's testimony. She is trying to fight with everybody, telling them they are disrespecting Mr. Wesson and that they need to leave; the kids are not theirs.

Meanwhile Elizabeth asks Sofia to come talk to her near the rear of the bus which is closest to the road. This would divert Sofia's attention away from the scene of what is happening in the house; Marcus is still standing at the doorway. Sofia, having previously lived in the Wesson household, is suddenly very fearful of what could happen; she continues to keep an eye on Marcus. After the conversation with her aunt, it is then when she realizes Marcus is no longer in the doorway, and her aunt, Elizabeth, is also on her way, into the house. Officer Nelson's attention is diverted from behind him when someone yells, "She hit her in the stomach!" It is Ruby holding her abdomen area; she was arguing with her mother who then punched her in the stomach. Concurrently happening, according to Nelson, is two young males walking past him, going into the residence just for a few seconds, where someone tells them, "Stay out of this. It's none of your business." The two males walk back outside—these males are never identified. Officer Nelson is still trying to calm down the commotion and arguing behind him, dealing with who hit Ruby. Marcus is slowly walking toward the southeast bedroom; this would be the last time Nelson would see him.

Simultaneously while the Ruby incident is happening, after talking to her aunt Elizabeth, Sofia, panic stricken, runs to a police officer who is on a cell phone and asks him to go into the house and get the kids. Ruby begins to hysterically panic as well, feeling that the children are in danger because Marcus is out of everyone's sight. In despair, Sofia runs to another patrol car and asks them to go inside of the house, but that officer tells her there is nothing he can do without a search warrant.

Sofia and Ruby finally run up either side of Officer Nelson, yelling and screaming hysterically that Marcus is going to hurt the kids. Nelson can only see Kiani moving what seems to be coffee or end tables to the doorway of the southeast bedroom. Sofia then hears two shots. Brandy, standing in front of the house, hears two muffled pop sounds in succession like her sister Sofia. However Ruby, who was farther away from the house, claims she heard six shots earlier—she would be the only one to hear that many shots March 12th. Not finding a solution through the authorities, Sofia frantically runs for the doorway of the house, but it is too late. Serafino, the son, is running out; behind him is the main mother Elizabeth; her cousin Kiani and sister Rosie. They all have the look of horror on their faces, blank with white fear. Nelson yells to the sergeant that they have a problem on their hands; he then proceeds to enter the home at this point, asking everyone else to get out of the house. Since the sergeant has his hands full, dealing with a bunch of people outside who are arguing, Nelson goes in solo. He then calls for Code 3 assistance: meaning, officers to respond and come to the scene with lights and sirens. The time is now 3:30 PM. Nelson, about 15 feet into the living room space, proceeds down the hallway to the bedroom door; there is no sound, no babies crying like he had heard earlier.

Meanwhile, outside the house, Sofia grabs Elizabeth to find out what happened, everyone is screaming and yelling at each other—the sisters, cousins and support group relatives Ruby and Sofia brought with them. Hearsay comments fly out of the mouths of Serafino and Elizabeth: "I think dad killed—dad shot Lizzie and Sebrhenah," says Serafino, according to Sofia.

"It's your fault!" Elizabeth screams, falling apart over the scene that has just occurred.

Sofia hears the threat from Kiani that she is next, feeling that

Sofia is responsible for what has just happened in the house. Sofia starts screaming, as well as Ruby; eventually Sofia passes out. Ruby later tells the officer how she felt Kiani made death threats to her and Sofia; now they were both worried about their physical safety.

Waiting for back up, Officer Nelson is still inside the house. He asks Marcus to talk to him, assuring him no one is in trouble; he still gets no response. He calls out to him four or five times in a loud voice—nothing. He bends his ears carefully, hoping to hear the crying infant he once heard earlier; it is silent.

Shortly thereafter, three or four other officers come on the scene and Nelson backs out of the residence and takes a position at the front doorway of the house and stays there for a while. About ten other officers arrive on the scene. After another officer takes over his post, he then leaves the house to get more information on the situation, approaching the group of relatives they moved across the street, away from the front of the house. A nephew of Wesson steps up to talk to Officer Nelson about the situation; he tells the officer that Marcus is like the guy from Waco; that he has multiple wives. He also tells him that his uncle carries a .22 handgun. He informs the officer that Marcus will probably kill the children before letting them be taken. Nelson then walks up to Sergeant Jackson and gives him this information. Based on that information, Sergeant Jackson calls for the SWAT team; asking for negotiators.

By 4:10 PM, Nelson is asked to go to the command post at Olive and Delno—about 100 yards from the scene—and brief them on the situation; Marcus Wesson is still inside the house.

Finally Nelson receives the information at 4:49 PM that Marcus surrendered and had been taken into custody.

Nelson then precedes to the rear of the residence, where there is a wood fence, a gate, and there is a door on that side of the residence along the window. He then pulls off some of the six foot fence pickets, which were nailed to the frame, so that officers could have a better view of that side of the house.

It was the scene after the arrest of Marcus Wesson that startled members of the police force and distressed family member:

Officer Eloy Escareno, a police officer for eight years, was one of the officers dispatched in regards to an officer requesting Code 3 assistance at approximately 3:29 PM. He also testified in the preliminary hearing April 8th, telling the courts that when he arrived he said he witnessed several people outside yelling and screaming and officers attempting to calm them down. He was briefed on the situation and then positioned himself 40 to 45 feet toward the front door with Officer Kurt Smith and Officer Jimmy Passmore. It was then that Officer Passmore made reference to the coffins inside the house. Escareno leaned in to see them.

After an hour and 20 minutes, Escareno said Marcus came to the front door. He commanded Marcus to place his hands in the air where he could see them, not to make any furtive movements, Marcus responded and followed his direction. Then Marcus very calmly, quietly pointed to Officer Passmore and said, "I need to talk to you." His hands and clothing were soiled with blood.

Escareno told Marcus, "Listen to me, you don't need to talk to anybody at this point." He then ordered Marcus out of the residence; instead, Marcus began to step back deeper within the house. Escareno told him, "Stop, do not go backwards, come forward and just continue to listen to my voice."

Marcus replied, "You're going to hurt me." Escareno assured him they would not and to just follow their commands. Yet still a second time he pointed to Officer Passmore and said, "I need to speak to you. Come here. I have something to tell you."

The Murder Scene

Marcus then stepped outside the house and was taken into custody. Escareno then entered the residence, proceeding to the southeast bedroom; he would be the first one to enter the dim lit room, followed by officers Passmore and Tello

Escareno used his flashlight to pan the approximately 10 by 14 foot room that was too dark to make out anything. He then saw something to his left on the floor that he glanced at quickly. When he took a second glance, someone turned on the light; he noticed the bodies…the first body appeared to be the oldest or tallest from his point of view and she was positioned face down with her feet closest to the door and head closest to the east wall. In shock, Escareno immediately dropped his shotgun and dropped to his knees, yelling out to the officers to call for Code 3 ambulance. As his eyes panned further along the wall, he observed six to eight other bodies intertwined. He couldn't distinguish what leg was to which body because of the dripping blood that masked the interlinked body parts that formed a pile from top to bottom, oldest to youngest— the infant was at the very bottom. Without moving the bodies he stuck his hand through the body masses, using the carotid method to check their pulses and got nothing; on his observation, the blood had not coagulated, the bodies were still warm. Because the infant was too young, he checked the brachial pulse on the arm as well as attempting to find one on the neck. He began to cry because he realized that they weren't going to find any—or he wasn't going to find any live bodies, so he stopped. Shortly after, Officer Passmore also began to check for pulses after Escareno and found no life.

Disturbed by the tragedy of the scene involving the children, Officer Escareno left the room, leaving Passmore and Tello to inspect the rest of the scene; his job was done. Escareno wrote a four page report about what he saw and the events that transpired before Marcus's arrest.

To make sure no neighbors or family members entered onto the property, Escareno stayed another 25 minutes before leaving.

When Officer Passmore testified in the preliminary hearing on the same day, he said after the arrest he conducted a pat-search on Marcus; he verbally told him he had to check for weapons or knives. Marcus told him he had a knife that should be located in his lower pocket on his leg; he had it for 28 years. Passmore found the knife sheath in the pocket where Marcus indicated, and he then proceeded to detain his hands using multiple handcuffs. After that he went into the house and rechecked the pulses after Escareno.

Although Passmore had his statement taken from him by Detective Reese, he, himself, did not write a report. He did try to dictate his report about that day, but it didn't take.

Michael Harris, who had been an officer for almost 31 years, also gave testimony the same day as Escareno and Passmore. He was the detective in the homicide unit that was called to the scene at about 5:30 PM. He was briefed by officers Passmore and Smith of the multiple victims involved. Harris went to the southeast bedroom and noticed three coffins on the north wall, a dresser, a chair, a baby's crib and another piece of highboy or armoire furnishing. He then noticed the bodies piled into the northeast corner of the room in a 4 by 4 foot square area. He had first counted seven bodies, but later counted nine; they all had suffered a gun wound to the face. Under the adult victim, Harris witnessed a hunting-type knife with a five-inch long blade. He also noticed the two older victims, 25 year-old Sebhrenah and 17-year-old Elizabeth Jr. were lying somewhat to the side, but their arms were stretched outwards over the top of the pile. The firearm was located under Sebhrenah's body, specifically her right leg. Harris waited for the photographs to be taken and then shortly left the bedroom scene.

Later detective Reese had given Harris a family photo to show to Sofia who identified all of the deceased family members. Harris would write a 13-page report regarding the crime scene.

One major scene was noted by almost all police officers who testified in the preliminary hearing; they noticed that Ruby and Sofia were very emotionally shaken and upset over the loss of their children. Kiani and Rosie, were unemotional, unmoved and very calm to have each lost two children—a peculiar scene that had many baffled at the obligations of motherhood versus victimization.

Later on the autopsies would be performed by Dr. Venu Gopal who showed Harris the x-ray on the light board where the bullet entered the right eye, traveling in an upward direction to the brain. All the victims except for one were shot in the right eye; Sebhrenah's child, Marshey, was shot in the left.

Carlos Leal, Jr., who had been a police officer for 14 years, assisted Detective Reese with the investigation and with some of the interviews of the family members; this is where their investigation truly began.

Inconsistencies with Testimony

The defense noted that Sofia never warned the 15 or so people she brought over to Marcus's house on March 12th of the suicide pact. Nor did she tell them about the older children at the house plotting and planning to do anything in reference to a suicide pact, to prevent the younger children from going with the law enforcement. She also never told them that as along as Marcus could be seen in clear view, everything was okay; otherwise, there could be danger if he got near the children. Nor did she explain to the officers on the scene his religious belief that could be detrimental to the lives of several children trapped in the house; the cops never asked Sofia why she didn't. The defense also that is was odd that she did not tell the police that she saw the oldest child, Sebhrenah, with the leather pack that carried Marcus's gun. The police never followed up at the scene to find the leather pack in question as evidence.

They also felt there were inconsistencies with Sofia trying to pry open the door with physical force, and then still not being able to get into the room; there was no lock on the door, they argued.

Could Sofia have been so traumatized that she would forget to tell the police valuable information in regard to the family's religious beliefs, relating to mass suicide? Or was she still protecting her sisters, cousins and Marcus from any harm, stuck in the old fear Marcus taught her; that law enforcement would take all of the children away? It is hard to believe that Sofia said nothing, and not so hard to believe that she would say anything according to the conditioning of her thoughts by Marcus; she was taught to believe the fears he created for her. In fact, although newly away from the household, Sofia still had ties and fears; she kept very obedient to the Wesson family's wishes not to try to take Johnathan and to help the family in their greatest time of need.

The defense said what was also conflicting is the demeanor in which they described Kiani; the police reported that she was calm and unemotional during the whole interview, however Sofia and Ruby both attest that she made threats to them about taking their lives. The behavior does not match the statements. Ruby and Sofia were to be the ones known lashing out at everyone, even in front of the six chaplains.

Finally, another inconsistent perspective was Ruby hearing six shots; she didn't mention it at all in the first interview. She stated that fact the second time she was interviewed by the police. The defense felt that Ruby was embellishing her story because of the hatred she had toward the Wesson family.

The Defense Doesn't Rest

In referring to the physical altercation Sofia confronted when she walked into the house, it was with Sebhrenah, who yelled the obscenities at her first, telling her to get out of the house, according to the defense. There in the living room they began to physically fight, pushing and shoving each other, yelling and screaming at the top of their lungs. Soon it was Sebhrenah who would retreat to the southeast bedroom; the front door of the house was open, with Marcus standing there. The defense questioned why the police, who were standing outside, hearing the altercation, never went inside to stop it?

There was also a question of the 15 people; what were they there for, if they weren't there to stop the fighting? If Sofia's testimony is so, that she got into an altercation with Sebhrenah, why didn't any of them step in to stop it? What was their purpose, to stand around and watch all these things happening before them?

According to Ruby's testimony later, a counsel had suggested that they take a bunch of family members as support; they could possibly get their kids without getting the police involved. So the group of uncles, brothers, wives, girlfriends of the uncles and brothers were to follow the plan she and Sofia had set: Sofia was to go inside first, they were going to try to get Marcus outside and have the uncles and men keep him occupied while they grabbed their children to leave the Hammond home. The plan reversed on itself; Marcus began to retreat into the house because of the group of people surrounding his house.

When it comes to the autopsy report, there is nothing in the report that shows evidence of malnutrition, Sofia's main complaint for trying to get her child in the first place. The defense noted that the police had already seen these reports before sitting down to interview Sofia; they never questioned her as to why she told them in the interview that they saw no evidence of malnutrition.

The defense was also baffled by Sofia, who had once been stabbed with a knife by Marcus, at how she was not afraid to get her child, she was not afraid of Marcus at all. They were suggesting that when someone has been assaulted by a person, they normally aren't brave enough to go back and confront them again without some sort of fear.

Then there was Officer Nelson: Why didn't he question who the two gentlemen were that walked passed him to go into the house while he was standing at the front doorway talking to Marcus? Not only that, but when the nephew of Marcus told Nelson what was going on, he never asked him his name, nor how he knew the information regarding his uncle and the .22 handgun.

Also, in the initial dispatch to Nelson, there had been mention about a gun and neighbors said they heard shots around 2:30 PM: this was just as Nelson was arriving on the scene. For the defense, the gunshots already heard implied that Marcus couldn't have been the one who pulled the trigger; the problem was that Nelson never interviewed any of the neighbors for clarifications on who heard the shots, per the cross-examination by the defense during the preliminary court hearing. (Although statements from a local newspaper who interviewed neighbors would confirm gunshots heard around 2:30 PM that day or earlier.)

Kiani's Truth

For a moment, it seemed as if there was a dashing hope for the defense; maybe all of Sofia's statements to the police were lies, Ruby's too. Could it be that all of the preliminary hearing was imaginatively created by Sofia and Ruby who were distraught because they wanted their children, whom they would never see again? Did they hate Marcus and the Wesson family that much?

It wasn't until the confessions of Kiani Wesson did some of Sofia's and Ruby's stories begin to match Kiani's statements.

Douglas Reese was the homicide detective who had been a police officer for 17 years. He became the lead investigator in this case who interviewed Kiani in the early Saturday morning of March 13, 2004. He found that Kiani, born April 23, 1977, had lived at the 761 West Hammond street address for the last seven months prior to March 12, 2004. She also listed the other people living in the house at the time: Elizabeth Jr., Sebhrenah, Rosie Solorio, and the seven younger children.

Kiani told detective Reese that she was inside the house when Sofia and Ruby showed up to their door. She went to make a phone call when she saw Sofia coming into the house. She asked Sofia what was going on, and Sofia told her that she came to get her son Johnathan; Kiani told her no, that she couldn't do that, and that they had agreed to leave them with the family. Sofia's previous statements in regard to what happened when she entered were all validated by Kiani who also confirmed that her sister/cousin Rosie blocked Sofia from getting Johnathan. Kiani then said all of the children were taken to the southeast bedroom by her, Rosie and Sebhrenah while Marcus was near the front doorway. Marcus was trying to calm everyone down and keep others out of the house. Marcus didn't want the children taken in this manner.

Kiani said that everyone continued to fight while the officers stood in the doorway; one of the officers said that CPS (Child Protective Services) would be called. Marcus then agreed give Sofia and Ruby their children, but he didn't want to do it in that manner; he wanted to talk about it. Marcus was still trying to get Sofia and Ruby in the house.

Eventually Mr. Wesson left the front door and went into the southeast bedroom where Sebhrenah was. Soon Kiani said she heard what she thought was a gunshot or a pop noise from inside the room, and when she heard the noise, she turned around and left the house. Kiani's two children, Illabella and Jeva, were killed inside of that room.

The Arguments of Death

In a closing argument, public defender Pete Jones felt that the evidence presented at the preliminary hearing did not demonstrate that Marcus Wesson shot and killed anyone or ordered the killing of anyone on March 12th, he said, "it was too speculative." The evidence is that he went back in the room," said Jones. "Officers heard no shots fired after he went back in the room."

Jones continued that the gun was found under Sebhrenah: "The wound that was inflicted to Sebhrenah could easily have been a self-inflicted wound, based on what the Court has heard, based on its trajectory," explained Jones, who also pointed out that a knife was underneath Sebhrenah as well—none of the interpretations were pointing to Marcus Wesson as having killed the nine individuals in the room that day.

Jones also felt that basing the truth on the two nieces' testimonies was very biased, for they had already preset in their minds that Marcus was the killer.

Still in his statement to the Court, the evidence was lacking, and the defense was at an extreme disadvantage because they didn't have the audio or video tapes, which they felt could have been copied in an hour or so and provided to them weeks prior to the April preliminary hearings.

"We didn't have those (the tapes) to review to see if we could impeach," said Jones. "But I think even what we had heard and raised here, there's a certain vagueness about this and it would—it would bend due process beyond the constitution here to—to find that all this—these requirement have been met by the prosecution."

Jones felt Wesson's defense had been severely compromised by the manner in which the case had been undertaken.

Meanwhile, Prosecutor Gamoian obviously felt differently: consistent with Mr. Wesson's teaching of these children from a very, very, early age—so she commented in her closing statement—she felt that it had always been his belief, which he taught all of the children in the household, that it's better for the children to be killed than for them to go to CPS or for law enforcement to become involved with the family and break them up. She felt that because his teachings over the years, it was consistent with the March 12th murders in question.

"Nothing happened until Mr. Wesson went to the room. Everyone believed that everything was okay as long as Mr. Wesson was in sight. The children were safe," explained Gamoian. "…only after Mr. Wesson entered the bedroom were any gunshots heard." Marcus stayed in the backroom for so long—an hour and 20 minutes—before surrendering himself to police, that it seemed odd that he wouldn't be involved in the process of the killings.

Gamoian also pointed out that when Marcus was taken into custody he thought he had a knife. Low and behold, the knife in question was found underneath the children; she surmised that this knife was lost during the nine counts of murder that was occurring.

On the accusation of not providing the defense with adequate discovery, Gamoian said that all of the discovery they had currently available had been provided to the defense; she couldn't see how they had been prejudiced.

Jones then appealed to the courts that the children were already shot by Sebrenah Wesson, who Sofia earlier saw reaching in the leather pouch where it was known there was Marcus's gun, also noting that no gunshots were heard by the credible witnesses—the police. Ruby, who was farther away than the police, claimed she heard six shots. He insisted that her state of mind was in jeopardy because she was so hysterical over the situation. Also the inconsistency of everyone hearing a different number of shots: Kiani who was closest, heard one; Sofia, might have heard two; officers closer to that room, never heard a shot.

Weeks later after the preliminary hearing, Jones stated in the court documents that gunpowder residue tests show Wesson was clean. This would mean that there was another shooter all together: Sebhrenah Wesson. This would be the best defense for Jones and Torres to convince a jury of Marcus's innocence: he didn't fire the gun that killed nine of his children. This would put a whole somewhere in the prosecution's case; Marcus was officially not the killer.

Explaining Gunshot Residue

How powerful is the evidence of gunshot residue? Powerful enough to free an accused who otherwise would have been convicted.

The question of how this fact affects the case is enormous; gun shot residue cannot be wiped off or avoided by wearing gloves when firing a firearm.

Jeffrey Scott Doyle, a Firearm and Tool Mark Examiner

Forensic Scientist Specialist since 1979 and who received his bachelor of science degree in police administration and associate of arts, Criminalistics, stated on his educational website: www.FirearmsID.com the following in relation to the pattern of gunshot residue:

Pressure building behind the bullet is released when the bullet exits the muzzle of the firearm.

The bullet acts like the cork in a shook up Champagne bottle. When the bullet exits the muzzle, pressure behind it blows the gunshot residues out of the firearm's barrel under high velocity. The residues are expelled from the barrel in a smoky cone shaped pattern.

The amount of lead residue emitted from a gun can vary slightly from shot to shot. Fouling in the barrel from previous shots can slightly increase the amount of lead residue emitted from one shot to the next…gunshot residue can be deposited on articles of clothing when in close proximity to a discharged firearm. *But will it stay there?* In most cases the answer is yes.

The various elements contained in gunshot residue are not readily water soluble and clothing left exposed to the elements will not usually diminish the residue deposits. Other factors such as heavy bleeding and rough handling of the garment can cover up or dislodge some residues. This has to be taken into consideration when conducting all such examinations. The garments must be promptly collected, allowed to air dry, and packaged in a way that will minimize contamination.

The clothing submitted to the laboratory will be examined to determine if a pattern of gunshot residue is present and there are a number of examinations conducted to aid in this determination.

With all of that said, we must take into account the influence of Marcus himself...

According to renowned criminal defense attorney Ernest Kinney, who has tried various high profile murder cases and won, said in a personal interview that Marcus could be proven just as guilty, whether he was the shooter or not, "Even if he's not the shooter... if he's the one that the prosecution can prove that commanded it, ordered it," explained Kinney, "he was like a Charles Manson, then he would go down on murder, just like the shooter. You would face the same penalties. You could not even be present at the scene but be the mastermind, and you go down on the same murder case as the others. So that's where we are there."

Kinney also said that the prosecution's greatest defense would be that Marcus was the lone man standing after the murders that occurred in that one room.

"The key argument they're going to make is that the only one that came walking out of that bedroom that day was Marcus Wesson. Everybody else was lying in a heap. And their position is going to be, either he was the shooter, or he commanded the shooting, because if he didn't want the shooting to happen, he could have stopped it. He's a big man; he could have taken the gun away. That's the argument. Prosecutors are going to harp on two things; he's the only one that came walking out of that room alive and number two, look at his physical size, look at his general big nature; he's a threatening type person, he's evil, convict him. I think that's where they're going to convict him."

As the story built itself based on familiar but crude obscurities as told in this chapter, more bedlam was to follow in the aftermath of murder, described in the next revelation.

Morality is of the highest importance - but for us, not for God.

~Albert Einstein

"For out allotted time is the passing of a shadow, and there is no return from our death, because it is sealed up and no one turns back."
~ Wisdom of Solomon 2:5; *The Bible*

Revelation 2

The Aftermath

Squared off with yellow police caution tape, the former murder scene was massed with foiled balloons imprinted with youthful phrases and colorful balloons that trailed the Hammond house corner. Teddy bears, stuffed rabbits and other toys with faces sat up with gleaming youthful looks, waiting to be held by the child who wasn't there.

Candles burned for the lost souls, lost bodies that were part of its eternal flame. Wax drippings cried permanent tears, overflowing and caked on the sidewalk as a remembrance of the tragedy.

Nine crosses glistened in the sunlight, twinkling light for their youthful children that have passed on, engulfed, surrounded and protected by the Mother Mary candles in colorful arrays.

The blood that dripped on the sidewalks when the chaplains carried the bodies out from the house stained the memory forever into Mother Earth whose asphalt ached; until they were eventually washed away, so that sorrow and guilt could no longer lay their beds in the hearts of this sunken neighborhood. Families would have to move on after such a hideous sight. The infamous case would go down in Fresno history with sullen regrets, questions unanswered, and fear of the unknown, forever.

Spectators tempted by curiosity came to the site as if they were at an amusement park with the masses of people and tour groups; until they got there, it was a massive memorial service for the eight

761 Hammond office-house space shaded by trees, once the grounds for murder.

Photo by Johnny Sharp

The side of the Hammond house, pathway to the backyard, can easily be mistaken for a small office building.

Photo by Johnny Sharp

Pots and pans and a barbecue like stove are worn and rusted

Photo by Johnny Sharp

Barred windows are stringed to the wooden fence with yellow string in the backyard.

Photo by Johnny Sharp

children, one adult, gone from the Wesson home.

Members of the community, with hearts extended to the grieving, raised money for the expenses the family could not afford following a nightmare they never thought would unfold. Yet in the still of time, there was a moment of silence, reminding everyone that life is not promised forever.

On this corner at 761 Hammond Ave., life was lifeless; it had no more tears to drown in the sorrows that succumbed a community in shock. People related to the deceased children; and people who had children cried because it could have been their loves lost, their pride and joy involved in the confusion of entangled relations, emotions and violence. Younger onlookers compared their age to the Wesson children and stood with cold blank stares.

There were no more talks of who was at fault, only of what will happen next? Who will take care of the families now? And, why did he do it; did he—Marcus, the trusting father—do it? These questions surrounded the mystery of the household and family that stayed silent as hermits in their private cave, only letting the immediate family be privy to their way of life. Now, the whole world was watching, the whole world was a part of this family, the whole world wanted to know more.

The media swarmed the neighborhood, and the people of the community with the news of the Wesson family absurdities, nomadic lifestyle and eccentric behaviors. Meanwhile, there were still nine funerals to be performed; the focus then stood on the families in mourning.

It would be the Jesse Cooley Funeral Home who would offer their church services, including the caskets, for free. They felt that this would be their way to give to a community that was also mourning a compounding loss. However, they would only handle seven of those funerals; Ruby and Sofia would have their children Aviv Dominique Wesson and Johnathan St. Charles Wesson buried together in Clovis, Ca.; their graves would have no headstones due to the lack of money—they would be known as the secluded Solorios.

On the other hand, the Wessons, the surviving mothers and their family supporters, had an outpour of assistance, something they would never understand until after the funeral, until after real life hit. Pastor Paul Binion would be the presiding reverend that would witness the turmoil, the upset, the family confusion, the grieving.

A Fallen King

Being around for a long time, Rev. Binion was accustomed to services that involved mass killings; gang banging, murder, the real difficult ones. However the situation Mr. Cooley was bringing him into was so extreme, the Cooley staff was concerned he might not do it.

"I knew and they knew that it was going to be a media circus; killing own children, incest aspects," said Rev. Binion in a soft calming voice.

Confident about his ability to perform the service for the Wesson family, as he reviewed the program of what would take place at this mourning session, he found himself perplexed by the women who sat in front of him. He witnessed uncanny looks from Kiani, Rosie and Elizabeth, just barely grasping the true reality of what happened. In an hour meeting, he felt the emotions, pain and confusion of a family losing its king.

"They wanted me to get a feel, meet with them for over an hour. I had been doing this a long time—I had no trepidation—I counted three very frightened women, amazingly, very close knit; they were each other's support system, wife, daughter, niece—all had children by the same man," said Rev. Binion.

Slowly, slight truths trickled through the threads of time that seemed to stitch the missing pieces together. The three Wesson women were fair game to an apathetic society, nation and world.

Pastor Binion recalled: "Their concern was, 'Where from here do we go?' Mentally, they were out of control. I gathered from them they never went to public schools, they were never allowed to watch TV. 'Society won't understand it: this is normal for us, not for other folks, but for us.'"

"I didn't' sit in judgment; I felt sorry for them, they looked lost. I asked them where to from here: 'We Don't know.' They were unaware of public assistance. I didn't feel resentment for Mr.

Marcus Wesson

Wesson; they felt he was taken away from them, and they didn't understand that."

Why did they avert their eyes? Their line of sight kept falling to the ground. Without question it was a sign of shyness, reclusion, a sign of being untouched by the outside world and its civilians.

"They couldn't look at my face, they had a hard time looking at me. They would hold it for a few minutes, then their heads went down," said Rev. Binion. "The daughter (Kiani) was more outspoken, she more readily spoke up."

And now, the service would begin; the world would be watching from the outside with peeking cameras and cued mics. Rev. Binion wanted to assure them that he would be there for them and at the same time, the service would be a media circus outside of the church. National news media blanketed the streets, waiting for a moment of truth to explain it all. Rev. Binion explained the circus sight:

"I was told by someone that Channel 30 was the only one allowed in there. There were police there and the media was gathered up and down the street taking pictures, flashing cameras, but they were not allowed inside the chapel."

According to Elizabeth, she requested no cameras be allowed at the open-casket service, she was shocked to find them there and inquired about their presence. It would be a Cooley staff member that informed her they only allowed that certain television station because they needed proof for their records and tax purposes to write off the donated funeral expenses. Hidden in the back would be a television camera, taping the grief-stricken family members. Elizabeth would not be happy with this manipulative behavior she did no understand at the time. (We asked for a statement from the Jesse Colley Funeral Home in regard to this accusation—there was no comment.)

As the hearse pulled up, the show began: Rev. Binion readily met the family who rolled up to the curve bewildered and saddened. What would be more disturbing would be the scene inside—the open caskets.

Custom made bus, designed by Marcus Wesson, is a one-of-a kind transformed motor home with showers, couches, bathrooms and other amenities.   Photo by Ken McC

The mystery of the coffins baffles the community as rumors circulate of vampirism. Ten coffins were confiscated from the home March 12, 2004.
Photo by Ken McC

As the Fresno community mourns, they await answers, in defense of the deceased Wesson children who no longer have a voice.

Photo by Ken McCoy

"When I got there, there were open caskets, that's what I saw," continued Rev. Binion, "everyone was shot in the right eye—the short caskets for babies, it was heart breaking; I had to prepare them for this; 'It's going to be a difficult scene for you, seeing ones you love.'"

The Service

Thirty family members congregated in the church of sorrow. Pastor Caldwell read scripture, immediate family members were very open with their emotions, receptive; they broke down, they wept and cried for an hour or so, according to Rev. Binion. Mothers grasped their dead babies from the caskets and held them in their arms, wishing for their souls back one more time. One more hug, one more cry. The great mourning had begun.

There was a son of the main mother Elizabeth Wesson who Pastor Binion described as more in control of reality and saw this as a tragedy that they had to move on from in a short period of time. The problem was Elizabeth didn't know what to do from there.

"The mood of the family was one of just uncertainty, fear, acceptance, but then nonacceptance, but I didn't notice any hostility, bitterness. (He was still 'dad, father.') When Mr. Wesson was spoke of, it was with endearment," commented Rev. Binion.

After the service, the family was swept away and they took the caskets to the sanctuary and allowed media into the lobby of the Jesse Cooley's Funeral Home. Pastor Binion was hit with the media right away, speaking to them of the courageous open-casket service of the seven dead Wesson children. As soon as he stepped outside of the church, there was more media; he remembered friends calling from around the country about seeing him on CNN and other major television stations.

Describing Elizabeth

A mother who has lost her dethroned King fights for understanding, direction; living with worries she never had to encounter before in her life. Now, they were coming, problems Marcus normally handled were piling up, accumulating day by day.

"Elizabeth seemed to be a woman who hadn't developed self-esteem, she was totally dependant upon him. He controlled, dictated, ran the shots. His sons loved him, respected him. Most people I know detest their fathers," according to Pastor Binion who has treated members of the community that were molested by their fathers when they were younger.

"His (Marcus's) authority was not in question." Pastor Binion said. "The family felt that 'the choices he (Marcus) makes has always been in our best interest.'"

Confused by the tragic slurs, blame would be the only solace for Elizabeth, Rosie and Kiani.

"It was very clear to me that the two nieces that decided to report him (Marcus) to authorities; they are definitely considered the enemy," expressed Binion. "They felt they were the cause of what happened, and that this would have never happened, 'If these two had shut their mouths, we would not be in this situation today.'"

Lost in despair and the details of like, Elizabeth and her family were not sure where to go, who to trust and where to call home; a home that was now a murder scene. A home they could no longer run to for peace.

Who Really Knew?

"A tragic thing—this is how the community should feel," declared Binion. "The family of Wessons knew what was going on, but they didn't report it. So I said, if I knew of persons in my family, you know, I wouldn't report that? I urged the public, if they knew of things in their own families, report it. It seemed like with the Wessons, daughters, nieces, it was like, 'This is the way we are, our father, he was our leader...'"

"I met Elizabeth's sisters whose daughter had children by Wesson: how come she didn't say something? Call the authorities? Why didn't she raise them (her own children)? And she allowed this man

The coffins were said to be of a special imported sturdy wood, good for making furniture, according to Wesson family members.

Photo by Ken McCoy

FRESNO
Nine bodies found in home

CALIF.

Sacramento

San Francisco

Fresno, California

Los Angeles

San Diego

170 miles

Police Chief Jerry Dyer, appalled by the scene, speaks in a broken voice, fighting back tears after attesting to one of the worst mass murders in Fresno's history.

Photo by Ken McCoy

to have children with her own daughters? So you (Marcus Wesson) sit there, just spreading seed all over the family, just taking advantage of those girls' trusts. If you want to go the Old Testament, you'll see many situations like this (where they marry their second or third cousin); but the populations were much smaller."

Pastor Binion remained in a shock state when pondering reasons why family members did not report the family sooner—they all knew but said not a word...

"Elizabeth's sister, husband, somebody that was close to them should have intervened, 'Hey guys, let's cut this generational thing.' But see it's not generational, his parents are pretty normal. This was a situation that was allowed to go on. He (Marcus Wesson) exercised mind control and definitely controlled their thinking. What ever he told them, they took as gospel—If you keep your family in isolation, then you dictate everything you say."

The seven bodies were cremated at the Belmont Memorial Park in Fresno.

Confusion and Misreported Facts

Through all of the grieving, there was a family at a loss for words; the new world preyed on their fears, making them snippets of reality. The funeral services were over and now the real chaos would begin.

It was known that the community raised over $1,700 for the families involved in the slayings. At least $1,400 was donated to Elizabeth and her family to pay for the flowers and funeral expenses; $314 to nieces Sofia Solorio and Ruby Sanchez to pay for their children's expenses.

Unfortunately, money always seems to bring problems; Elizabeth's brother Mike felt that Elizabeth was going to use the donated money for Marcus Wesson's defense. Elizabeth said immediately upon reading this in the newspapers, she turned the money into the police chaplain, furious at her brother's misleading statement to the media.

According to Fresno Police Chief Dyer, Elizabeth spent $1,400 for food and other expenses since the slayings and that an additional $400 was given to her to help her through the rough times. The remaining $600 was put into a Bank of the West account for the children of the Solorio and Sanchez family. Consequently, Elizabeth said this information was inaccurate, she returned every dime of the money and suffered through bad times without almost anything. In fact, she was sent a bill from the Jesse Cooley Funeral Home, who had stated in the local media and on national television that they would pay for all of the funeral services and burial arrangements. However, this would be the same funeral home that would try to get the funeral for the seven children paid for through a victim's rights organization who said they would not reimburse the funeral home because they had already heard Jesse Cooley Funeral Home publicly state that they would donate their services to the Wesson family. Elizabeth slowly began to lose trust in people of the community who claimed they wanted to help her family. (Jesse Cooley was contacted repeatedly on this matter but did not make a statement refuting Elizabeth's claim of being sent a bill for the funeral expenses.)

Although the event is not related to the March 12th crime scene, about a month later the Jesse Cooley Funeral Home burned down; there were no suspects found for the arson.

Left to the side of the road like leftover dinner, the immediate Wesson family members not only felt betrayed, belittled, and left behind because they still were supporting their incarcerated father and husband, Marcus Wesson, but they also felt the sting of angry community members who could not accept their unique lifestyle which people felt hindered the Wesson children.

Elizabeth, who sought help for living quarters for her remaining family, was only accommodated in a low-rated, dangerously situated hotel; $600 a month was the stipend provided by Fresno County social services that would only last for one month; all of the money went to the daily cost of room and board. There would not be enough for food, gas and other basic necessities. Constantly harassed, hounded and threatened by the outside community, who were confused with the actions of the murders in relation to the family; they were all persecuted at this hotel because of one family member accused of murder: Marcus Wesson. Elizabeth had to get her family out of there; her exotic looking, beautiful daughters were threatened and even sent letters from men who saw their stunning beauty on television. Frightened by such behavior of onlookers, she moved to a temporary concealed location for safety. Elizabeth sought help from the victims and witness service of the courts who informed her that she would not be able to get assistance unless she would be testifying in court against her husband, Marcus Wesson. Elizabeth did not see this as an option for her, her daughter and niece—Rosie and Kiani—and her youngest son Serafino.

Elizabeth and her family were soon cut off from social services because they would not reveal their new living quarters; Elizabeth would continue to use the 761 Hammond as her home address. The $600 was no longer issued after the one month. At this point, Elizabeth and her restructured family were in dire straights. They attempted to move back into her 761 Hammond Ave. house as a last resort. However, it became no resort as Fresno City and County officials would inform her that the tiny-three room housed was zoned for commercial property. There would be a fee to change it from commercial to private property which she obviously could not afford.

Desperate to find a place to live, she even looked to her Santa Cruz property which she and Marcus bought back in the 1970's, with the hopes to someday give the property to their children. However, she could not leave the county because her passport, (she was born in Mexico) had been confiscated, but the Santa Cruz land was in jeopardy and under new ownership, according to Elizabeth. The arrangement they had with the original owner of the land involved them making $500 dollar payments every month; the male owner died and his son took over the situation. With Elizabeth not being able to make payments when they were due because Marcus was in jail, the new owner denied that the land was owed to them and was able to sell the property without Elizabeth's consent for $500,000— there was no official record to prove that Elizabeth and Marcus had been making payments on this property. She only had receipts that were on their motor-home bus, which was impounded and could not be retrieved.

Devastated by this news, Elizabeth whirled in lost hope in her faith and a worsening family condition. The world she knew was falling apart right in front of her eyes; yet, there was more to come...

The family would have to wear the same clothes as that night of March 12th; everything was confiscated and taken into police custody: passports, birth certificates, clothing, the motor-home bus and all that was on the bus. Elizabeth said she asked to retrieve her passport, her receipts for the Santa Cruz property, and some clothing for daughters; they were denied. The prosecution was still gathering evidence from the items they collected from the murder scene. Also, somehow Elizabeth was given misinformation in regard to her things in police custody; she said there was a threat made to her by one of the detectives who said she would have to pay storage fees unless she made statements against her husband, Marcus Wesson. Believing the threat, Elizabeth felt intimidated and discriminated against by the courts and began to slowly distrust the court appointed victim's advocate for the family. She slowly backed away from any assistance by the county who she felt harbored conditions and expectations. It was as though she was stuck in an inescapable trap.

A simple trip to the grocery store was a freak show for the community who would spit, make jokes and criticize the surviving Wesson mothers. Elizabeth felt that she could go nowhere in public without being recognized, especially with her children who were very noticeable because of their outspoken comments in support of their father to the media. Their look was so unique, anyone off the Fresno streets would know who they were.

Feeling that everything was stripped from known existence, she began to feel the pressures and reality of her situation. Now the problems began with the media reports of her family.

Surrounding neighbors on 761 Hammond Ave. reported that when ever they saw Marcus outside with his children, they were seen wearing all black, with head scarves and long sleeves, walking 10 steps behind their father in public. According to Elizabeth, she never knew any of her neighbors, rarely saw them and said they made up many allegations regarding her family's life style.

Other neighbors reported to the media about the foul smell that was a choking odor at night—rotten meat being cooked on a grill in their backyard was the culprit of this nauseating stench. Still many other witnesses discussed their rummaging through garbage bins for cans and bottles to turn in for a little change and going to Mc Donald's dumpster to find thrown-out hamburgers.

It became evident that Fresno community members and others outside of Fresno began to depend on the 11 o'clock news or tidbits from newspapers of the background of Elizabeth and her family. What was more disturbing to Elizabeth was the accusations continually reported about her husband Marcus; the continual report that he was the killer; technically wrong information. It would be *The Fresno Bee* newspaper that would straighten out such information, but not the surrounding media who took the information and ran with it; the public specifically knew Marcus to be guilty of being the shooter, he was already guilty even though it hasn't been proven.

As previously stated and noted, in the court hearing after the preliminary trial by Public Defender Pete Jones that Marcus Wesson was not the official shooter: Jones reasoned that the children were killed before Mr. Wesson ever went into the room. Such significant evidence is truly scant in the visual media which focuses on Mr. Wesson being the actual assailant of the nine murdered victims. During the standoff, the police talked to Wesson from his doorway. At a moment of distraction, Wesson then went to the backroom where he stayed for 80 minutes before surrendering. Although these officers who had surrounded Wesson's home did not hear any gunshots, it ultimately became Judge R. L. Putnam's ruling that there was sufficient evidence to uphold judge Lawrence Jone's order to have Wesson stand trial. However, Prosecutor Lisa Gamoian argued that several members of Wesson's family heard gunfire, the question would have to be, when? Gamoian said, in *The Fresno Bee* May 21, 2004 article that, "Nothing happened to the children in the bedroom until Wesson left the doorway." The problem with this statement remains; when would Wesson have shot the gun if the police never heard any gunfire? It was finally noted later that his 25 year-old daughter, Sebhrenah Wesson, was the actual shooter who was responsible for the eight deaths, and then her own. When the bodies were found, her body was found on top and to the side of the stacked bodies, where a gun and knife were found under her body, according to police testimony. This signifies that the daughter fell on these weapons after then killing herself, according to Jones.

There were more revealing facts from the crime scene that were turned into a field day for the mystery-solving crime sleuth or curious mind that wanted to know the sensationalized truth of the coffins and links to vampirism. It was noted in the media that the 10 coffins found at the crime scene were for the nine victims; people surmised that Marcus threatened his children with death and placement into the coffins if they did not obey them. Others felt the family slept in the coffins as vampires, seeming more like a family awake at night because of the constant noise and banging neighbors would complain about, as the family was working on their bus or house.

Elizabeth and her family were inflamed by news reports of these inconsistent statements about her family. She remarked that Marcus was a very handy man and could turn any scrap wood or metal into anything; the coffin was of an exotic antique imported wood they planned on using to make furniture for her daughters. The only link to vampires was Elizabeth's was her love for reading Ann Rice books; an alternative New Orleans author celebrated for her gothic writing style; erotic, unusual sexual episodes; horror/fantasy stories, often about vampires, mummies and witches; stories with sado-masochistic themes and passionate, distinctive characters set in Old England or older times. In fact, Rice is known for her books that have turned into movies: 1994, Neil Jordan directed motion picture Interview with the Vampire, Queen of the Damned, and Exit to Eden was starring Rosie O'Donnell and Dan Aykroyd. The police, fearing that such evidence could be crucial to defining the case, confiscated all of Elizabeth's Rice books. Elizabeth reassured us that she was the only member of the family who read those books; not even her children were allowed to read them, nor did they know. She unfortunately found it ironic that the coffins and the link to her books were a possible connection to anything relating to her husband Marcus.

The motor-home bus had its own stigmas as people were told there were hot spas and secret rooms for Marcus to perform his sexual acts in private. However the motor home bus was designed for sleeping quarters for both the girls and boys who slept in separate areas. As later discussed in detail by witnesses who been inside of the customized motor-home bus, the vehicle was known to have showers, a bath tub, bathrooms, a kitchen and living quarters. There was also a room to perform the births of the children so that medical equipment on hand would be available; this could have been mistaken for a spa or pool room.

Finally, there was the mistreatment of the family when they were first taken into custody for their statements in relation to the crime. Kiani, Rosie, Serafino and Elizabeth were immediately separated and interrogated by the different detectives individually. Elizabeth said that she was intensely interrogated for 10 hours straight, from the night of the murder to about 7:30 AM. She said she was so distraught and shocked, grieving because of the murder of her children she could not focus on giving the police accurate information and continually asked for legal assistance; she said they denied her. According to Fresno community activist for underrepresented minorities and a criminal defense attorney, Leslie Westmoreland, some minority civilians are unaware that they do not have to make statements without the presence of requested legal assistance. As a result, they may perjure themselves due to lengthy questions that are confusing or misleading. Such was the case with Elizabeth and the rest of her children interrogated. They were unaware that their rights were violated; she and her children only knew that she was to answer all questions asked. Westmoreland also said that the police do not have to officially tell the civilian making the statement that they are entitled to legal assistance; in their eyes the civilian making the statement is doing his/her duty to report what was witnessed at the crime scene. The police were doing their job finding out who was responsible for the nine murders.

Some had sympathy, some had disgust; the Fresno community was slammed into its own perception of the reality, wanting to know more about the Wesson family, their life style, and where they came from; answers we find in the next revealing chapter.

It is always too late, or too little, or both. And that is the road to disaster.
~David Lloyd George (1863-1945)

"Nothing is secret, that shall not be made manifest; neither any thing hid, that shall not be known."
~Luke, 8:17; *The Bible*

Revelation 3

Getting Down to the Roots of the Wesson Family

They were a quiet family, not much in the public eye, away from public notice, living a good, simple life; so they felt. Then murder happened, making them one of the most infamous families to ever live in Fresno; a simple walk down the street by any Wesson is now noticed by everyone. Before, their long walks down the Fresno streets were quiet, unnoticed, and almost innocent.

Their so very private lives are now pried open unwillingly. This invasion amplifies the disgrace caused by the media's outspoken truths, making the shock more intense for these family members who can relate best to the world Marcus Wesson once created for them. This was a world made through the visions, ideals, fantasies and dreams of Marcus; now fading away as a distant memory. The Wessons could live no longer under the radar with the presence of the tragedy that hit their lives. So how did a family of a quiet, concealed nature become so reveled in the Fresno community?

San Jose, Ca. is as far as one can go to find some of the roots of Elizabeth Wesson who moved there from Mexico when she was around six years-old. She was then known as "Elizabeth Solorio." Marcus Wesson was in his 20's when he met Rosemary Maytorena Solorio in her 30's—a 13 year difference—Elizabeth's mother. They cohabited and had a son together in 1971; Elizabeth, almost a step-daughter to Marcus, was about 11 years old. Rosemary had carried on relationships with two different fathers creating nine children before Marcus Wesson came into her life.

With a very sheltered life, Elizabeth's first encounter with black people occurred when she moved to the east side of San Jose at approximately six years-old; referring to them as "dark people," not knowing how to describe them. She remembers growing up and not having much, and her brothers always into trouble. It wasn't until Marcus came along that order and structure were brought to the home. Soon all of the children in the household, including Elizabeth, were pulled out of school and were home schooled.

Elizabeth attended school until the 7th grade, remembers an old acquaintance, Connie, who moved to the East San Jose neighborhood in 1970. Connie remembers her childhood friend Elizabeth as being very shy and withdrawn and yet calming and strengthening to her own spirit. Living across the street from the Wesson family, Connie said that her father and Marcus Wesson would have long talks about God and became very well acquainted with one another; Connie's dad was a minister. As she was going through her own trauma of being sexually abused by her own father, Connie often confided in Elizabeth for strength.

"At school, I was really shy, but she was always with me, you know," said Connie about Elizabeth in a May 24, 2004 news interview with KFSN, Channel 30 in Fresno, Ca., "she seemed pretty confident, we sort of stuck together."

"When we weren't in school we were always together; we would be outside talking or in her house. I don't think she ever came to our house very much, but I would go to her house a lot," reflected Connie.

It wasn't before long Connie and her family found out that Marcus was in fact married to Elizabeth, not her mother, Rosemary Maytorena Solorio. This struck Connie as a mistake because she was baffled to realize that Elizabeth was married to Marcus at such a young age.

"I remember when I found out about it. My dad was talking to Marcus; talking about God together. Marcus said no, that he was with Liz. I was only 11 or 12," said Connie in a personal interview who then moved away from San Jose nine days before she turned 13. She also said that once they found out this information, she didn't see Elizabeth much, and she didn't see her at school; Connie never got to see her again.

However, when confronting Elizabeth with her childhood friend, Connie, she did not recall being the best of friends with her nor did they play together. Elizabeth said she remembered feeling sorry for Connie because of the trauma she was going through with her sexually abusive father who would also make Connie's mother stay inside of the house all the time. Connie's father would threaten to beat her mother to death if she ever stepped foot outside. Elizabeth also noted that it was rare for them to play with the neighborhood children.

Strangely enough, Connie remembers catching butterflies in coffee cans with Elizabeth and the other neighborhood children. She remembers Elizabeth being quiet, as well as the other girls in the family; while the boys were a little bit more active and much more vociferous.

"They (Elizabeth's brothers) played with my brothers…running around, riding bikes, scooters, typical boy games," said Connie.

Not remembering much about Rosemary, Elizabeth's mother, Connie remembers the kind, gentle manner of Elizabeth.

"I don't think I ever heard Liz's mother talk, Liz was really quiet; she would talk to me, but always in a whisper, very soft gentle voice," said Connie, who considered Elizabeth a very nice, warm and special friend. She also felt that Marcus raised Elizabeth to believe whatever he is, whatever he believes he is, and that the murders had nothing to do with Elizabeth and her character.

Three years after the birth of Marcus and Rosemary's child, there is record of her daughter, Elizabeth, marrying Marcus Wesson in 1974; she was 15 and he, 27 going on 28 (they married three days before his 28th birthday). It was just four months later that they bore their first child Dorian—a boy—, and three more children thereafter: Adrian (male), Kiani (female) and Sebhrenah (female.) Before moving to Santa Cruz during the 1980s', they had another boy, Almae. Once moving to Santa Cruz, they bore their son, Donavan, who died at six months old from spinal meningitis. Thereafter

Marcus Jr, Elizabeth and Serafino were born in Santa Cruz. Finally, the youngest of the group, Gypsy, was born in Fresno County. *(For clarity, refer to the genealogy chart of the "Wesson Extended Family Web," located towards the beginning of the book.)*

Before we go into the nomadic lifestyle of the Wesson family or any eccentricities connected to them, it would be crucial for one to first understand the life and background of Marcus Delon Wesson.

His current stature of 5 feet 9 inches and 300 pounds is accented with long, graying, unproportioned locks that barely brush the back of his knee, intertwined with sporadic, unlocked new growth that almost stands as an afro. His shapely, bush-beard streaks shades of gray, white and black around the trim, extending to the opening of his nostrils. The hard lines flow down his cheek bones depicting the hardships and disappointments of his life. His calming, yet mysterious droopy eyes hypnotize a blank stare that pierce through those who talk to him one-one. As each lock hangs in its own distinctive fashion, the public whispers of this look to be that of a potential killer, a man to be feared. Neighbors on 761 Hammond confirmed this fear. His astute posture and aloof stance create his giant demeanor, making members of the community tremble.

In the San Jose, Ca., newspaper article, of the *Mercury News*, a Fresnan shaken neighbor said, ``He's (Wesson) a type who could see right through your skin, your body, clothes," said Barbara Alec, 61, who has fearfully encountered Wesson on the street.

Perhaps this was the intention of Wesson, beaten by life itself; yet, having the power to put strangers in fear because of his appearance: a large, plumped black man with evil looking "dreadlocks," a nice tumble of laughter to break from the normal beat of life for Wesson; he, himself, was noted for finding humor in such naiveté, according to Lois Dugovic, who owns the antique store where Wesson bought the 10 questionable coffins about five years from the date of the crime.

"Wesson seemed aware people were scared of him and that made him laugh," she said in an Associated Press news article.

On a public forum website, *Websleuths Crime Sleuthing Community*, dated March 13, 2004 at 11:14 PM, in a threaded discussion, a person wrote, "I am shocked and disgusted. He also is a VERY scary looking individual whom I'm sure I'll see in my nightmares."

One could compare the judgments of appearance to moments in history, where those who did not conform to the norms of society were ostracized: Salem Witchcraft trials of 1692; African-Americans during slavery and the Jim Crow era; those blacklisted for un-American activities during the 1930s'- 40's by our own government authorities; people of Middle-Eastern descent or with the last name of Muhammad after the 911 attack on New York's Twin Towers. One of the biggest flaws of human nature is to judge a person by appearance; everyone has standards and a set of beliefs that form their views on what is normal and accepted.

Ironically, underneath the sensationalized physical appearance of Marcus Wesson and public opinion based on these, impressions, he certainly was not—is not the man portrayed as a monster in the media and by the Fresno community, according to some of his family members.

"The Marcus Wesson on TV I don't recognize. That'snot my son," explained his elderly mother, Carrie Wesson who now resides in Washington State. "The Marcus Wesson I raised was a brilliant, loving, God-fearing child," she continued in a LA Times news article, March 19, 2004

Marcus Delon Wesson was the first born to Carrie and Benjamin Franklin Wesson in Kansas On August 22, 1946; they soon moved to San Jose, Ca. Carrie and Benjamin also had three other children—another son and two daughters—who did not want to be identified nor comment on their brother's case. Because of the previous still birth before Wesson was born, both hard-working middle-class parents showered him with plenty of love, and strong Christian beliefs that reflected the Seventh Adventist background, according to his mother.

Carrie Wesson explained that Marcus's entertainment was the church. "He wasn't running around seeing what little girl he could catch," his mother said. "Instead, he'd be at the table eating food, always stuffing his face. That's why he got that big," said the LA

Times news article.

Devoted members of the Seventh-day Adventist Church—worshiping on Saturdays—and keeping a vegetarian diet kept Marcus grounded; known to wear basic clothes and suits, he was a young teenager that never attended dances, but believed in clean-cut, short haircuts and suits.

According to a April 18, 2004 *Fresno Bee* news article, Marcus's friends remembered him wearing a white shirt, jacket and often a tie to Fremont Junior High School in the San Bernardino area from 1960 to 1961; while other kids wore jeans and T-shirts.

Charles H. Cox, an old classmate of Marcus, now a 58 year-old general building contractor who lives near San Bernardino, remembers Marcus being a "nice" and "great" guy who wasn't a bully and never picked a fight, according to the Fresno Bee article. The very studious Marcus sang in the junior high choir and enjoyed watching and building his electric trains. The *Fresno Bee* article explained that old classmate Kenny Brownfield, who now resides in Florida, lived a few blocks away from Marcus and had been over there once or twice and remembers the many trinkets and electric trains at his house. Classmate Cox said he and Marcus would watch freight trains pass through town and trade H-O model trains.

Known for his unique ability to build anything out of nothing, the LA Times news article went on to explain the typical young boy who was simply talented.

"Members of his family recalled the boy born in Kansas who could put together intricate puzzles that confounded adults, who constructed go-carts and electric cars out of parts picked up at flea markets and passed on this love of building to his children…In his teenage years, her son (Marcus) began to build all sorts of motorized vehicles out of shopping carts and scrap metal."

One customized vehicle caught the eye of an engineering professor at Stanford, said his mother, "I know I'm bragging, but this professor asked Marcus where he got his training to build it. Marcus told him he didn't have any degrees, no formal education beyond high school.

He told him, 'It's a gift from God.' "

Marcus was known to be very compassionate as stated by his mother: he cared for lizards, snakes and toads and once found a dog left for dead in a trash can. "I told him, 'That dog's dead,' but he wouldn't believe me. 'Momma, I can hear a faint heartbeat.' He fed it milk all day and night and brought it back to life."

It was evident that such ideals then spilled on to Wesson's children later on, according to the LA Times article:

"My dad wanted his children to make something out of nothing," said his oldest son, Dorian Wesson, 29. "If I wanted a toy, he'd buy the wood and supplies and tell me to use my imagination and create what I wanted."

As far as education, it is on record of Marcus attending the San Bernardino School District from 1960 to 1965; by 1964 he was a junior, but did not have enough credits to graduate; although, he did enter the Army, serving from June 22, 1966 to June 3, 1968, according to the same *The Fresno Bee* article.

"Classmate Cox said: 'Most of us joined the military because if you didn't, you were going to be drafted.'"

Army records show that Wesson received medical corpsman training for 10 weeks in 1966 at Fort Sam Houston, Texas. According to a 1970 summer *First Team Magazine* interview of Specialist 5 Bill Manning, a 2nd Battalion, 8th Cavalry medic, students learned a panoply of subjects at the Medical Training Center (MTC) in Houston, with the curriculum ranging from basic physiology to how to sweep a hospital ward. Included were the sterile techniques for handling necessary equipment, and how to administer the whole array of injections. The largest single area of instruction was in the administration of bandages and dressings and the consequent treatment of wounds. The use of splints, burn treatment, and different forms of artificial respiration were also part of the course. Treatment of shock and the heavily circumscribed use of morphine were two other areas of importance.

"The program seems to be designed with an eye toward the field medic rather than the hospital orderly. With classes running from 8 a.m. to 5 p.m., it seemed more like a high school than the Army, even if the men were going to war," said Manning.

According to the article, at the end of the course the medic is prepared for what the Army thought he would be running into in a war setting.

This extensive training would explain why Marcus never really attended a doctor or hospital to birth any of his children or for any sickness or health issue; he had former knowledge from his medic background.

After such intense training, Marcus became an orderly and driver with the 695th Medical Ambulance Company, stationed in Europe from Nov. 27, 1966 to Feb. 6, 1968.

The Fresno Bee April 18, 2004 article continued to explain that Marcus returned from the United States on June 2, 1968 and spent four years in the inactive reserves. Morgan, an Alabama cousin, described Marcus as a homebody who didn't drink, smoke, or do drugs.

However, when he returned from the military experience, things would never be the same again for Marcus.

In the aforementioned LA Times news article, Marcus's mother noticed the grave change in his political views, "During the Vietnam War, Wesson was stationed in Germany and came home with a different political outlook," she said.

"We always liked nice things, nice furniture, but Marcus said we were too materialistic. He got married and kind of dropped out," she recalled. "I wouldn't say he became a hippie, but he had some of that hippie lifestyle."

Upon finding his way back to the states, Marcus moved in with Rosemary Maytorena Solorio into the three-bedroom, single story house located in the lower-middle class areas of east San Jose. Rosemary had just separated from an abusive husband; Marcus was a breath of fresh air who became immediately loved by the family. He was known to bring order into Rosemary's children's lives, spending a lot of time with them, and was very kind and friendly.

So where and when did things go wrong? What did Marcus see during wartime that may have skewed his hopes, his dreams, and his thoughts of the American society?

Or, what racism could he have encountered as a black man that tore this sheltered man's views apart from what he grew up knowing?

Whatever it was, Marcus Wesson's soon to become mysterious turn of views created the most mysterious turn of events that others would not consider normal according to societal standards: the nomadic lifestyle, the extreme views of God that played a role in the Solorio/Wesson family's core beliefs, and the incestuous web that seemed to tangle around religion, manipulation, and thwarted beliefs.

It would have been nice to be able to ask the incarcerated Marcus Wesson these pivotal questions; however, visitation hours are no longer allowed with the approaching trial set. However, the other mysteries concerning the specifics of this case baffled the public and will finally be revealed in this next revelation.

> *If you don't know [your family's] history, then you don't*
> *know anything. You are a leaf that doesn't know it is*
> *part of a tree.*
>
> **~Michael Chrichton**

"Forsake not an old friend; for the new is not comparable to him: a new friend is as new wine; when it is old, thou shalt drink it with pleasure."
~ **Old Testament Book of Ecclesiasticus** *9:14; The Bible*

Revelation 4

The Way They Were: Family, Neighbors and
Good Friends That Knew Wesson

Neighbors: we don't seem to recognize them until something awful happens; there they are, peering through the windows of our lives; judging us on what they see through the windows and what little they may have known of us.

However there are other neighbors that surely remember us through our kind hearted actions or sobering get-togethers flailed with laughter and fun—those would be the neighbors we all want. For when something bad happens at our residence, they can be there to support the unbiases of judgmental situations…could they still be unbiased if the accusation dealt with murder?

San Jose Living

Before the Wesson family ever thought of Fresno, they lived humbly in an eastside San Jose, Ca. neighborhood where everyone knew everyone. The neighborhood consisted of black and Hispanic lower class and lower-middle class families who were happy to get by in life with humor, fun and good neighbors.

As the children would roam freely on their bikes, racing each other down the street through the neighborhood or playing kick ball in the streets; an impression was being made on one youth who came to know Marcus Wesson. His name was Alex Garcia; he was only 10 years old at the time. Now 39, Alex Garcia, a truck driver, from San Jose, Ca., lived on Harriet Avenue in San Jose, Ca., the same neighborhood of Marcus and Elizabeth Wesson.

They were the sole match together—Marcus and Elizabeth—a match made in heaven in their eyes, no evidence of incest just yet; except for the queer move of Marcus dating Elizabeth's mother first and having a child with her. One might say although he was not married to her mother, Rosemary Maytorena Solorio, he would have still been engaging in incestual relations early on with his potential step-daughters: Elizabeth and her sister Rosemary Solorio; of course then marrying his potential step-daughter Elizabeth. All in all, these behaviors were not displayed to an extreme then as they are now; Marcus's bizarre sexual rituals he performed with his blood daughters were to come many years later.

In San Jose Marcus lived with his family in a house in back of another house; a tiny one-room shack they called home—it was just the baby boys, Dorian and Adrian Wesson, living and being raised with the church-abiding Wesson family values. To the outside world they were poor; to those that knew him like Alex, they were a happy family that had all the comforts of the rich due to the added love and pure-life living of the household. There was a lot of clutter around their house because Marcus would go to flea markets and buy stuff or go to garage sales and buy something cheap and sell it; he wasn't organized as far as nice furniture. He built his own stereo—"one of nicest stereos you could hear," exclaimed Alex—own speakers, and his own cabinets; Alex explained that everything was just old furniture—nothing new or fancy, just a comfortable, old little shack, that one could imagine back then, they probably only paid $100 or $200 for rent, according to Alex. Liz (Elizabeth), of course, was said to be on welfare at the time. Marcus would do his regular wheeling and dealing to survive and bring a little income—reminding Alex of the old 70's television sitcom *Fred Sanford and Son*.

Introduced to Marcus Wesson by a friend, Alex remembered his friend ramping and raving about the roller coaster in Marcus's backyard, a cool bus, and the fun games they would play over there, "It (the slot car track) was two layers, and we had a big old track, it wasn't just one of those circle ones," described Alex, "it was a big track and we used to sit there and do 500 laps—we were down like we were doing the INDI 500, we would sit there for four or five hours."

Alex soon developed a friendship with Marcus that entailed more than just playing games.

"The man I once knew was a Christian, church-going man, that to me seemed very happy with his family and his two boys," explained Alex. "...he was a very smart man, very, very smart. To me, I thought of him almost as a genius, he new everything from just his math, his literature, his electronic skills, his history—you name it, he knew it. He was just a good man."

Marcus was known to hang around other male youths such as Alex, in the presence of his wife, Elizabeth. He would often preach to them about the Bible and ways to stay out of trouble. Soon Alex's parents began to worry about the 30 something year-old Marcus who was hanging around children less than half his age. Alex questioned Marcus, himself, curious as well; "So I asked Marcus, how come you hang around younger people? He said most people his age either drank, smoke, cussed and he didn't want that environment around his wife and his kids. He didn't hang around a lot of kids, actually it was two of us—the girls were too small, they were just babies. Liz always had the babies and we were always outside with the boys.

Everyone else—my sister, my brother—said something's wrong with this guy. As long as he isn't touching me, there's nothing to worry about, right? They said, 'Yeah, there's nothing to worry about.'"

What Alex remembered the most about his friend Marcus were the fun and games they would play at his house and the positive insights and values Marcus would role model to him and his Friend Tony Burnette; it would leave an impression on Alex the rest of his life.

"He had a bunch of games: we used to play monopoly; we ended up building a slot car track. I used to go to his house like 5:00 PM after dinner and I would stay there until one or two o'clock in the morning playing slot cars...Sounds kind of corny because by my age—13, 14—and I was still hanging around him, and my friends out there trying to mess with girls and get themselves in trouble, I would go to his house because it kept me out of trouble. We would drink sodas—no beer or nothing—play games...We would just laugh a lot, we had a lot fun, me and my friend Tony Burnett—

he passed away—he used to go over there also. We were cracking jokes, talking mess to each other; he was like my best friend, he was young at heart."

Till this day Alex is unable to comprehend the murders that Marcus was involved with; "For what happened I just can't believe it, it blows my mind—it's not the same guy. To me something must have happened to him in his life. He talked religious; I liked talking about Jesus, so that would get me going over there too. He knew the Bible inside and out so he would of course school me on that… Everything I could tell you is nothing but positive, there was nothing negative about the man that I knew. There was nothing unusual."

"I was broken heartened, shocked—you name it. I still can't believe it. (after hearing the news of what happened.) There was nothing he did wrong in my eyes, when ever he talked to people, it was just in a nice soft voice. He got along with everyone he met, in the six years I actually hung around him."

This would not be the only neighbor who would express Marcus's gentle religious demeanor and kind behavior towards others.

The Look of Marcus Then

In describing the look of Marcus, Alex remembered more of an afro—no dreadlocks—often dressed in sweats and T-shirts, known as just a humble kind of guy.

"He wasn't into fancy clothes, just kind of down to earth."

Alex knew Marcus as a big-boned man, not fat; "At that time I started working out and he would say I was getting pretty strong, I would make a little muscle, and I would ask him to let me see his muscles, he had these big old huge arms—he never worked out, he was naturally just big and strong. As time went on, he ended up getting a belly, big shoulders, big arms, big chest. It looked like one time in his life he must have did something; some people are just naturally born gifted and big."

The only time Alex recalled Marcus dressing up was for a job that lasted only several months; Marcus had told Alex he couldn't handle the bad treatment of others behind money, something he witnessed on the job as a banker.

One year he did surprise me…It was funny because he had this little car that had a big muffler on it and as soon as he came down the street I knew Marcus was home; I used to actually wait for him to get home, I used to hear the muffler sound and go wait outside so I could go play games with him…He used to wear a beeny hat, he had a big afro and he had to put a clothes hanger around it to kind keep it down and more firm. One day he came out of his car in a suit, a three piece suit, looking sharp. His afro nice and combed, a little part to the side. He had a nice black pin-stripped suit, a vest a jacket and some slacks with some nice shoes. I go what, 'What the heck is this, I never knew you had clothes like that,' He goes, 'I got a job at the bank,' I said, 'You work at the bank?' I think he worked for Bank of America or Bank of the West, I can't remember. He said, 'I gotta get a job, I was making little money so now I got a job at the bank.'

The Wesson family, for the most part, kept a vegetarian diet and grew mostly vegetables. Even Marcus's two young boys, Alex said, all they really ate was fruit –no candy. According to him, his kids were very happy kids, "They were little, of course, when I saw them from babies to four or five years-old, seven, eight years-old they were very healthy; he didn't let them eat no candy, he wanted them to be healthy."

Nice Voice Marcus

With the voice of an angel, as his mother once described, Marcus was always fond of music, especially as a child at two-years old when he would help find the gospel records for his mother. Alex and the people at the church witnessed the same talent of Marcus:

He was an excellent singer, when he was in the choir," explained Alex. "He sounded like the lead singer of the *Stylistics*, the high pitched voice… One day we were at church and he was in the choir and all of the sudden they threw that note in there, and the church was like, 'What? Who was that? That's Marcus, they couldn't believe it, that's your voice?'

We would listen to *Earth, Wind and Fire*; he could sing any song from *Earth Wind and Fire* and sound just like the record. He could make it (his voice) deep or high. My brother and his band, they were singing that song back then, and when Marcus started singing it, they said he could sing in my brother's band. But he wouldn't go to night clubs, of course. He said, 'I'm not going to night clubs, I'll sing for the church, that's it.' Marcus would stay faithful to his religious beliefs, not hanging out with men his age to go on drinking sprees or to hang out at clubs.

Ben Wesson, His Father

Alex only met Marcus's father a couple of times; he would come over and visit Marcus and the grandchildren once every six months. Alex remarked his clean-cut style of dress and fine jewelry and his striking resemblance to Marcus but a little bit thinner.

"He was a classy man; well dressed, he had a nice watch, nice jewelry on, a nice Cadillac—one of those long Cadillacs back in the 70s' …nice iron, creased silk, he had his gold on. It seemed like he would come by and visit Marcus, come see the kids and then he would just leave. When he came around I was there for a few minutes, but that's his dad, so I would leave so he could spend time with his dad and his dad could spend time with the kids."

Young Neighbors; "Cool" Bus

Yet there were other neighboring friends who were best friends with Alex and a few years older than him; they also knew Marcus— ironically they both passed away: one guy was hit, ran over, and the other one had a heart attack.

"After school we would always get together and end up going to Marcus' house," said Alex. It was in the early 70's that Alex would remember the good times on the customized motor-home transformed from a school bus; Alex and his friends would stew good times in the transformed shell that Alex often referred to as the "San Francisco bus."

"Every blue moon me and a couple of my friends would spend the night in that motor home." Alex described the unique details of the bus, "You walked in it and he had the couch on both sides and you walked passed that, he had a fire place and a card table, where we used to play games. I can still picture this in my head. And it was funny because you know back in the 70s' everything was kind of silky and groovy. They had a refrigerator, a stove a shower—it was like a motor home. A couple of times he let me spend the night in there, I would invite a couple of my other friends and we would just hang out and he would just say, 'okay then,' he would go inside with this wife."

Defining Friendship

The media would hunt the San Jose neighborhood on Harriet Ave. one-by-one, looking for those who knew the Wesson family; until, they came across Alex's mother, "My mom told the reporters, 'I know Marcus, he was my son's best friend, he was older than my son, but my son used to go over there,'" claimed Alex, quoting his mother.

"As far as him thinking he's my best friend—I don't know about that—but to me he was my friend, he never touched me, he never said nothing bad, never reared me in the wrong direction," said Alex. "When my friends started drinking beer and smoking weed in the 6th and 7th grade, I was at his house drinking 7-up and eating beer nuts, playing the monopoly. I didn't want to get in trouble."

Everything Seemed Normal Until...

It was not clear to Alex of when the normalcy left Marcus Wesson, during the several years he knew him. All he could ever see was the outpour of fatherly love coming from Marcus; nothing more, nothing less ... "I see Adrian in diapers, I see him always eating an apple. They got their little toys. The kids would be there, 'daddy, daddy,' and he would just answer the question, just like a normal father, like me and my kids like. You know, when I got my kids, I spent a lot time with them to help them become real men—everything was just normal.

As some would often judge "normal" as going out and having fun, this would not be the normal that Alex was talking about. He wasn't like a loner, but he kept to himself, he kept to his family. He didn't go out to night clubs; he didn't go out to parties. He would do a little shopping, he and his family—every Sunday they would go to flea market and they would come home with a bunch of fruit and toys and other stuff that he would buy that he could sell. He wasn't around a lot of people. As far as when I was around him or brought other friends around him he was normal—when it was just my wife, just my mom, just my sister he was normal—'Hey, how are you doing, nice to meet you…yeah Alex is a good kid, I hope you don't mind, he comes over.'

Considered his best friend, Alex would not know how to judge Marcus, who was charged with various sex crimes and accusations of murder.

"When I was in high school, he (Marcus) had moved away. He moved to Santa Cruz, we kept in touch, and I went to his house in Santa Cruz, and he had his bus up there and me and Tony Burnett used to go up there and visit him and just play monopoly—the same thing—play games, talk—it's a shame, I really miss the times we had. Of course, we grew apart, it's a little different now that I'm older. Just with what happened, I just don't get it…Until now, he was my best friend—but what he did, I don't have best friends like that."

For almost eight years Alex didn't hear from Marcus who moved to Fresno; Alex ironically had family that lived there as well. One day he suddenly passed Marcus up on the freeway…he had like a jeep; I passed up, I said, that looked like Marcus. So I actually slowed up. I was going almost 70 miles and hour and he was probably going 65 so I had actually stopped for him to catch up to me. Then I got out of my truck and he recognized me, so he pulled over. I had my wife and my kids, he was with Liz and his kids so we got out and exchanged numbers, gave a hug, asked 'how you been,' what a coincidence; it was fate or whatever, my friend I haven't seen in so many years, all of the sudden we run into each other on the freeway. Then two years went by and then all of the sudden he gave me a call, 'Hey how you doin?'

'I'm doing good,' I told him. He talked about his property he had by the ocean somewhere. We didn't see each other for quite a few years but we would talk; just to say hi … 'We need to get together and play a game of monopoly,' but it never happened. When Tony had passed away, that's when he came to the house because we had talked on the phone, I told him the bad news. He told me, 'I'll be at your house, I gotta come visit you and I gotta see what really happened,' because it was kind of like a fluke accident the way our friend Tony died, he just couldn't believe it, and that was the last time I seen him (Marcus) when he came down, that was about 2003.

Devastated Alex was simply looking for peace of mind, an explanation from Marcus, "It just don't add up—having sex with his own kids, I don't know where he lost it! Everybody I know loved him. What he did as far as—that's wrong, totally wrong, you don't do nothing to under-age girls, you don't touch. And as far as family members, you don't touch—that's terrible I just don't believe it."

Although hard to believe, there would be one more peculiar meeting that would stump Alex; Marcus's tone was very different when he saw Marcus for one more visit in 2003 when he came to visit him in Solata, a city right next to Modesto, Ca.

"He had two girls in his car and a son—he was 18—the boy came out, and he said, 'This is my son,' and I shook his hand and the two girls inside the car—that was the only thing that was kind of weird—I kind of waved to the two girls, they just waved but they looked kind of timid, they kept to themselves, didn't get out of the car and just stood in there."

When Alex asked Marcus about the beautiful, 18 or 19 year-old looking young women—one was light complexioned— Marcus told him they were his daughters and that one was his wife. Alex was in extreme shock;

"He told me, 'The Lord had blessed me with multiple wives,'

I asked him, 'Where's Liz at?' He said, 'She's still around, that's my main wife, my sweetheart for ever—you know me and Liz.' I asked, 'Is she okay with this?' To me it wasn't right. When I asked how old she was, I think he said 19. She was pretty—I said what's up with that, I'm 39."

Nevertheless, Marcus was still very polite to Alex and his wife; upon meeting her he gently shook her hand and introduced himself in a soft-spoken intelligent voice.

Alex couldn't remember any times where Marcus would treat

the girls different from the boys—that's why he was so baffled with what was going on with the rumors of his treatment to the women in the family. He couldn't understand where the rumors began once the murder happened.

"It's kind of weird because my friend Tony, he had a couple of sisters, and I guess one day my mom shared with me a couple of things they had said … like that he was controlling husband and he was rude to his kids, 'I said that's bullshit.' When we were playing games, Liz, she spoke, just like a normal wife would speak. She said her piece of mind. He never raised his hands at her, I never seen them once argue, she spoke her piece of mind. It wasn't like Marcus was in front and the kids and wife were 10 feet behind him. I heard a couple of people say stuff like that, I never seen that in the six years I lived across the street from them. When I started reading that stuff, I just think people tend to make things up. Of course there was a different side of them I didn't know. Liz was very quiet, soft spoken, also very shy. But when she had something to say, she would talk to Marcus."

The End Is Near

Alex recognized that Marcus was different than the average family man; Marcus was to an extreme, a Christian, who wanted to raise his family different in a religious setting inside of a corruptive, negative society, "One thing Marcus talked about was that the end of the world was coming, Jesus would be coming. He was always preparing his family for that. He didn't like scare me...we talked about the Bible quite a bit—he didn't harp on it a lot, he would mention that."

Still puzzled, Alex suggested that Marcus had to have been in a different but religiously logical mind-state when the pressure of him giving up his children to CPS arose.

"Maybe with all that stuff that happened, instead of anybody else having them, he wanted them to go to heaven."

Alex explained the rationale in the religious logic that Marcus would have used to compromise the situation: "You can't commit suicide, because if you commit suicide, you're like in limbo, you're stuck in between hell and heaven; that's one of the things he actually believed in too. I thought that maybe if he killed all of the kids—but he wasn't going to kill himself, so if he gets the electric chair (death penalty), they (the courts) kill him, then he didn't do it himself. Then at least he could be in heaven with his kids. He believes that one day he's going to see his kids."

Caught up, Alex felt that authorities were hip to what Marcus was doing with his own children, "He was worried; he wanted his sons and daughters to go to heaven before the law took them away."

Eventually the Wesson Family would move up and down the coast of California, almost as nomads living in the motor-home bus. In 1981, court documents stated that Marcus applied for the transfer of the welfare benefits to Santa Cruz County; he used the bus as his home; he was also reported living in a tent, a boat and in the Santa Cruz mountains. News reports would also state witnesses that would see the other vehicles that Marcus Wesson owned such as a boat, a van and a 1,700 square-foot home he built in Santa Cruz County from a $60,000 loan he obtained, according to *The Fresno Bee* April 18, 2004 article. Wesson also bought a permanent slip at the harbor in 1984.

Fresno Presence

In regards to the nomadic Wesson family, there were certainly neighbors that remembered their presence in Fresno. They were gypsies, modern nomads that could make a living out of nothing and do it very successfully—this would be the strong impression left on the Morris Family who lived next door to Marcus on Cambridge.

Steve Morris and his wife Gladys were missionaries of World Impact who moved to Fresno in 1985. They both worked in South Central with families before coming to Fresno and retired from ministries in 1995. Mr. Morris is now a vice-principal of a high school.

From 1985 to1995, the Morris family lived on Cambridge Street to start working with families there in need of assistance; for a long time that area had one of the highest crime rates in Fresno. It was home for a Fresno Bulldog gang that began their gang activities in that area.

"For a long time it (Cambridge neighborhood) was just avoided and left to deteriorate by the city," explained Steve. "That's why we moved in there and started working with families in there, and found out there were some really neat folks in that community that just needed a little assistance, a little direction to get themselves back together."

In the process of helping families, they met with the Wesson Family and became there neighbors around early 1990.

"We started doing some recruiting for our Bible club program around the neighborhood," continued Steve, "and we met Marcus and his kids and invited them to come out for some activities with us down at the building on Broadway. Marcus, I believe, came down once or twice to check out what we were doing, to make sure it was a good thing for the kids to be involved."

The reported close-knit family that didn't socialize with anyone would associate with the Morris family, becoming very close, according to Steve.

"My wife got to know his wife at that time, they got pretty close and shared a few things every now and then, you know, because my wife was trying to start a women's Bible study over there too… Marcus was just very friendly, I mean I'd be out in the yard working and I'd see Marcus…we'd end up talking. Again, our kids knew each other, and then the neighbor behind us, the three of us in the neighborhood just kind of became close to each other."

Right away Steve saw Marcus as a very unique being in that community; a father who was there with his children. Not knowing all the particulars about his family at that time, Steve saw Marcus as a devoted father who was committed to his family.

"We thought it was very cool that here was a dad that was staying around with his kids rather than running off and abandoning his family. So, the kids and Marcus were all pretty tight. Marcus was very creative with his children, spent a lot of time with them, especially the boys. I think he was trying to prepare them on how to handle being on a job, and to work with a boss. I mean the kids were very polite, the whole family was very polite. So, if you look at some of the external things, there are a lot of good things about that family."

The Morris children played with the Wessons and went to high school with the older children around 1994; Steve's son also took martial arts with a couple of Marcus's older boys for a while. The entire family was known to be very polite.

"That was another great thing that Marcus did…teaching his kids to be very respectful of everyone, not just people of position, but people on the street, gang members, homeless people. Marcus and his kids were always very respectful to various people throughout the community," said Steve.

Over a period of several years, Steve began to see a gradual change in Marcus and the Wesson family, making them more eccentric than usual. His usual ways and thoughts were transforming into something unrecognizable. A statement made by Marcus to Steve was puzzling, Steve was not sure what to make of it.

"The statement (by Marcus) was 'I'm thinking about getting my daughters artificially inseminated,' and we thought, 'What? What's going on?' I'd say 'Well why would you want to do that?' Marcus said 'You know they're pretty close as a family and they don't need to bring outside people in. They just kind of take care of themselves with that.'"

The Morris family became concerned about what was really happening within the family at this point, but they still continued to talk to Marcus; especially Steve, who would have long talks with Marcus about the Bible, philosophy and theology—the conversations would have no evidence or base to back up the estrange viewpoints of Marcus.

"He and I talked a whole lot about philosophy and religion—didn't have any real source of accountability in his theology to help ground him or keep him on track… Marcus and I would get in discussions again about what was the purpose of life, and God, and Marcus was always into the end of the world stuff, and wanted to be prepared. His thoughts seemed to drift more along that way. I always tried to bring him back to what we needed to do today was live our lives in a way that pleases God. So we'd get in these long conversations and go out and watch him work, and learned a few things by watching him use his wonderful skills he had as a craftsman."

Steve continued that Marcus would often focus on doomsday and the second coming of Christ, judgment day, and God's righteousness on the earth and him wanting to be prepared. Steve felt this was the crux of a lot of Marcus's theological thinking. Steve would always try to bring him back to where they were today, helping him focus on how would God want them to live for today.

The resourcefulness of the family was incredible; they always had resources but never the money; Marcus would do things in the community, bartering to get parts, food, to take care of his family. Steve recalled the craftiness of Marcus's work.

"He would trade his work services. Marcus was very, very talented; he is very talented. I could think of a few people that would fit that title of craftsman, and Marcus would be one. He could measure down to sixteenths of an inch on sheet metal and come out with accurate fits for welding and riveting things, and working with lumber, and carpet, and electrical. He just had that talent so he would go through different parts of the community and he would barter for some other resources, trade his work for some of the things he needed on some of the projects he was working on."

Marcus would pass down his skills to his children. "He would also have his family out there when he was working, his boys with him. His boys started getting part time jobs around the community and they were known as great workers. Just had fantastic attitude and any job they did, of course they did like their dad taught them…they did it right."

"His daughters were out working on the bus several times, and he was teaching them things. I think they made some of the curtains in there, the bus that they turned into a camper."

Steve was referring to the 80-passenger yellow, faded, worn customized school bus that took on a new look after Wesson's craftiness took over.

"I went inside a couple times when they were working on it. I was very impressed, he had all the seats out and he was welding up a special bathroom section in the back there. Welding on the floor, putting some walls up in there and he was trying to explain to me everything that he was doing but it was too complicated for me to get… They started really fixing it up, put curtains in. I believe after they got it fixed up pretty well they painted it and there was something he was doing with an old canvas, an old tent, a military tent. I'm not sure if he was going to put it on top to use it as a pop up on top of the bus to make it like another story, or if he was going to roll it out to the side, like a partition or an extension to the bus. So he got that old army tent somewhere by bartering again his services."

More and more Steve noticed the Wesson family becoming more isolated by the mid-1990s, so much that they just started to not come out as much, not socialize as much. No one thought much of this because Steve knew that Marcus wanted to protect his kids.

"We had a lot of gang violence and a lot of drug deals going on in the community and Marcus wanted to keep his kids out of all that. So, in one sense, it wasn't out of the ordinary not to see them. But in another sense it seemed like at the same time his philosophy became more isolated or eccentric also."

The living quarters of the Wesson family on 367 Cambridge was too an extreme, it would be hard for Steve and other neighbors to understand how they were able to cramp themselves into such a small space; Steve thought it was remarkable how they did it—a 100 square-foot upstairs space, about the size of a two-car garage, to fit 10 people.

"All the people in there, it seemed like it was always packed. Difficult to keep things organized, but they did a good job with it. Again, for what they had and where they were at, they did a remarkable job... It was shortly after 1995 that the city came in and shut the house down and his relatives lived up front, and they had to move out of the back too for code violations."

The once worn customized school bus they continually worked on was also a living space to accommodate the family. Marcus and his family would constantly work on this bus, pulling the seats out and rebuilding the bus basically from the ground up, "riveting, welding, putting in wood, water tank, just all kinds of special features that made it a first class camper bus," remembered Steve.

In return for Marcus's family being very polite to the neighbors, they returned the favor with kindness, supplying his family with basic needs.

"When they were fixing up the bus, they lived there. We had a neighbor right behind us, a Jewish family that got really close to Marcus and his family also, and they would let Marcus use their garage, their power, you know, any time he had a need. Sometimes it was financial, sometimes work, and Marcus would send the kids every now and then to our house and they would borrow money to go get ice cream to have a family night which we thought was really cool."

What Steve noticed before they had to move was the reclusion that started to become more apparent.

"Literally, they didn't go out except when they went to some of the activities with us or they went to the store. But after a while, even his kids stopped attending some of our Bible club activities and the whole family, for a period there, kind of became isolated. Then the boys moved out. I think they went up to Santa Cruz; they had a place there that they said they were working on…a boat or property that he owned up that way. They had a lot of resources and they were very resourceful for not having money."

Before the family became more and more closed in, Steve was not familiar with the recent comments from neighbors on Hammond Street who reported to the media that the women would walk 10 steps behind Marcus on outings, wearing all black.

"…Sometimes they were walking in front of him. They would go to the store, walk through the neighborhood, sometimes the girls were up front. At that time, again, we're talking mid nineties."

Marcus himself would wear dark clothes because of the type of work he was doing, according to Steve.

"But he wore work clothes most of the time. Towards the end there he started gaining more weight and I think he shifted to some other type if clothing, overalls. But most of the time it was just work clothes."

Times began to change; there were no more long discussion about God, the end of the world or the second coming of Christ. The puzzle of incest and family control just didn't seem to fit. Even the statement Marcus made to Steve in regard to artificial insemination was not taken seriously.

"…We didn't know if that was just Marcus having…some of his weird philosophy of keeping his family separated from the world. We had no idea it would be incest or abuse. That just didn't seem to fit what we knew of him."

Not able to put his finger on where things went wrong with the Wesson family, Steve could only envision what was going right at the time.

"They were on the right track of being a good concerned family but something happened. Not sure what all the things were that caused them to start becoming more isolated and to start separating themselves more and more from people and from the rest of society. But other than that if you saw them you would love to get to know them, you would consider them great neighbors. And the kids were just really great kids with my children."

In the next chapter, it is revealed why the Wesson family would become more isolated, away from a society that would not understand their ways, lifestyle and religious fondness Marcus would impose on everyone in his family. This would be the drastic change that would lead to murder.

Men will wrangle for religion; write for it; fight for it; die for it; anything but live for it.

~C.C. Colton

"Thou shalt not kill. Neither shalt thou commit adultery."
**~The Ten Commandment from,
Deuteronomy 5:17-18; *The Bible*.**

Revelation 5

Where Mayhem Began His Quest

For centuries man has discussed the end of the world or the second coming of Christ; however, this concept never became an issue until murder behind the Wesson name confronted its absurdity and judgment by others. It wasn't until then that people began to ask, "What in the hell is this end of the world thing? Did the man make it up to scare his family? How crazy is that!"

Well, it's just as crazy to know about history where Apocalyptism, belief that the world is coming to an end, was very common among many cultures and religious groups. Didn't Noah build an ark with this thought in mind, according to the biblical texts of Christianity? This was not an eccentric or outrageous thought in Jesus's time where even the disciples gave emphasis to the thought: the biblical writings of Daniel, Ezekiel and the Book of Revelation and most of the gospels are apocalyptic. When the disciples asked Jesus to tell them of signs of his coming and of the end of the world, it is said that Jesus replied: "Ye shall hear of wars and rumors of wars… nation shall rise up against nation, and kingdom against kingdom…the sun shall be darkened, and the moon shall not give her light, and the stars shall fall from heaven, and the powers of the heavens shall be shaken." (Matthew 24)

Jesus continued in Matthew, Chapter 25: "There shall be weeping and gnashing of teeth. When the Son of Man shall come in his glory and all the holy angels with him…and before him shall be gathered all nations; and he shall separate them one from another, as a shepherd divideth his sheep from the goats." From this day forth, many Christians have continued to seep their hopes into the second coming of Christ, considered the God of the Apocalypse. This became a common practice for people to dwell on, the life that was to come, rather than the life they were currently living.

Religious Antics

I remember many times my own grandmother—born and raised in Arkansas— constantly preaching to me about "living in our last days," and how I'd better shape up if I wanted to go to heaven. This was the mentality of a lot of older black grandmothers who had been through slavery, discrimination, oppression and Jim Crow; all there was to look forward to was death—in heaven they do not discriminate and everyone is treated with royalty, according to my grandmother back then; "Everyone is served milk and honey and are just as rich as the white folk," my grandmother would say.

As a child, I intently listened to my grandmother and became very fearful, hoping I was doing all the right things, so that Jesus wouldn't leave me on earth with all of the violence, the mayhem of Satan trapping souls and hell itself. I remembered how it changed my thinking of God, Himself, being a part of a cult that I had to be initiated into to save my own soul! I was even baptized, fearing that my ungodly sins during my youth of telling dirty jokes or playing pranks on my younger cousins would have the pearly gates shut right in my face: "You may not enter!" This was the voice that echoed in my head, as if it were God telling me I was too bad.

Over the years, I grew up, I was still believing this concept of me being less than perfect, doomed for hell; never did I know that technically my grandmother could be called a millennialist—I certainly was not familiar with this term and neither was she. However, I was aware that most older black people in my family and community felt and thought this way. I just don't think they knew that there was such a label; most people do not know the term "millennialist."

In the book, *Strange Sects and Curious Cults*, author Marcus Bach explained that most millennialist believe that Christ would descend from the skies in a cloud of glory and set up a perfect kingdom over which He would rule for a thousand years. He then explained that such people believed in a literal heaven and a literal hell and even the devil—just like my grandmother and many other friends I knew who grew up with similar teachings. The scene which all of these events were to come to fruition would be known as the Battle of Armageddon, where archenemies Lucifer and Logos would come head to head.

What's strangely fearful is not the way the millennialist or apocalyptists people may think, what's scarier is the forced discipline it causes anyone—especially a child—to follow. If this were a daily doctrine, practiced and hammered for two hours, as it was said Marcus would preach, one would have no choice—as a child—but to be fearful and dread dooms day. I know that my thoughts were constantly on what could I do right to make things right with the Lord. I remember being told that the devil was going to get me if I kept sinning: I literally would believe that a devil would come from the ground and snatch me out of my sleep. This fear I went to bed with—so did my cousins—almost every night when I stayed with my grandmother. Other friends who I have talked to have said the same thing in their experiences, to different extremes. Does this make their grandparents, my grandmother or parents who believe this and preach it to their children, bad people? No, I feel it only reinforces the power of religion because of people's fear of the unknown. When a person knows nothing else of the world but religion, I think that is when religion becomes a dangerous, manipulative tool.

The children in the Wesson household were subjected to this thought without a choice. If we were to blame them for following their father, a person who a child should be able to trust, then there is a fallacy and double standard for not only what I believed as a child, but countless other children. I hate to hear comments as to why the Wesson children couldn't see that what their father was doing to them was wrong—even the main wife Elizabeth married at the ripe age of 15—when that's all they knew, which was right to them.

It is no wonder as to why the Wesson children followed the enforced and invisible godly rules that led their lives, their actions and their beliefs. Some of things about to be revealed are not of the norm: my intentions are not to call this situation "normal" or okay. The purpose is to bring understanding as to what any religion can do to a person—none are excluded, justified or immuned, they all have a certain amount of power and control, whether conducted by a group or by individuals. We could have similar complaints about the oddities of the existing institutionalized religions; their beliefs and practices are all very different. Those aspects are explored in the next chapter.

For the record, although the Wesson family is known to have a Seventh Day Adventist background, the series of inexcusable sexual acts are not affiliated or assumed by the Adventist denomination. At the end of this chapter, a list of question-answer statements from the Seventh Day Adventist Spokesperson in regard to Marcus Wesson and the family members is included to defer any misconceptions about their beliefs and biblical teachings.

Preparing for the Worst

Vulnerability, innocence—taken at birth—no choice, silence, obedience were the identifiable traits the surviving Wesson children and wife Elizabeth displayed, all of them subjected to the confines of Marcus's world at a very young age. The hidden sex secrets would no longer be concealed, as a preliminary hearing would open a void of information, innuendo and appalling allegation.

In the same preliminary examinations discussed in the first chapter, the Honorable Judge Lawrence Jones, listened to a series of testimonies from police officials who recounted the video and audio tapes of these confessions by the surviving Wesson children and two Solorio nieces in question after the scene of the crime. Deputy public defenders Peter Jones and Ralph Torres against deputy district attorney Lisa Gamoian battled points of the testimonies and its authenticities for hours. Jones and Torres were certainly at a disadvantage because evidence they never received, although requested, was withheld. Tapes of family testimonies or other appropriate and essential evidence and discovery were never provided, making it near impossible to defend the client, Marcus Wesson. Jones continually argued that due process was not taken into consideration by the prosecution who would blind side them with new discovery, presented in the courtroom, which was never previously viewed by the defense. With Marcus waiving his rights to a speedy trial, the unprepared Jones and Torres were desperately seeking more time, in fairness, to be prepared for the grandiosities of this case—it never happened. In fact, the first day of the preliminary hearing, 33 more counts were added as alleged charges against Marcus Wesson, with no prior warning to the defense.

On a whim and a lawful prayer, Jones and Torres entered the courtroom for battle, yearning the right weapons but using only the tools they had. However, nothing could prepare them for the almost 400 pages of testimonies we are about to divulge, which included the detailed sex accounts of Marcus Wesson with his daughters and nieces throughout the years.

The Nieces Speak

Sofia's Story
Detective Michele Ochoa spoke to Sofia March 16, 2004 and presented her testimony in the preliminary hearing discussing Sofia's upbringing, first starting with the birth of her child she had, at age 21 in 1996, seeded by Marcus. Her seven-year-old son Johnathan—two days away from turning eight—was killed in the string of murders on March 12th. So how would it become that Sofina was not taking care of her own child?

According to Ochoa, Sofina was disowned by the Wesson family and actually left the residence—ran away— without the approval of Marcus or wife Elizabeth. Because of this she was not allowed to see her children or visit the family.

Sofia's birth mother was Rosemary Solorio, Elizabeth's sister. Sofia explained that she first met the Wesson family when she was nine years old, living in San Jose. It was at a church camp for the Seventh Day Adventist Church where she was introduced. She remembered them being very quiet and withdrawn. As she had attended public schools until the age of nine, Sofia noticed something different about her cousins who never attended public schools. Soon her mother moved them to Fresno where they began living at 367 North College Ave., her grandmother Rose Solorio's home. The Wesson family would often visit there. Sofia remembered their eating habits which she felt were strange: raisins, wheat, oatmeal and they ate very little meat.

In conversations with Elizabeth, may it be noted that she informed me of her sister's drug problem that was out of control, making it not feasible for Rosemary to take care any of her children; unfortunately, a few of her brothers on the Solorio side were the main drug dealers. This would be the reason that Elizabeth would care for her sister's children, according to her.

However, this did not stop the mediocrity of Sofia's memory of remembering meetings in the bedroom or away from her mother and aunt Elizabeth for extremely long periods of time—from morning to night—that included Marcus, Elizabeth and her mother, Rosemary. When Sofia was about 11 or 12, she remembered the Wessons living full time in her grandmother's house at the North College street address. Sofia recalled being gradually pulled away from her other uncles, aunts, and even grandmother. Her eating habits then changed, where less meat was consumed. Their religious background began to change, when she and her sisters were introduced to one to two hour sessions of prayer. If any of the children fell asleep, they were spanked.

Still living at the North College address, there were specific living arrangements at the residence: the grandmother Rose lived in the front house. There was a duplex in the back, which had a first and second floor. She, her mother Rosemary and the Solorios lived on the second floor, while Marcus and his family lived on the first floor. During the regular school year, all children were kept in the duplex. During the summertime, they would be able to come from hiding, sort of speak, and travel to Santa Cruz wherever their boats were kept in the Bay Area.

The daily Bible studies, which took the place of school, would last for several hours, with Marcus reading to them the King James version of the New Testament, and then preaching his interpretations of these verses. She said that Marcus would preach about the duties of a woman, which was to have children for the Lord before they go to Heaven. She was also to obey her husband. Marcus would present himself as the Lord to them and taught them that Christ had many wives, according to his interpretation of the Bible.

Also, when they were growing up, according to Sofia, they were taught to protect their children from law enforcement, if they were ever to come and try and take their children away. They were not allowed to let the law enforcement, or any other agencies, take their children, and they would have to do anything to protect them, so they were told. Sofia said they were taught that the fastest way was a gun, although the children were not taught how to use one, according to her knowledge. There was one incident she remembered while living in Santa Cruz , Tomalice Bay, on a boat. Her sister Ruby ran away and Marcus and Elizabeth went looking for her. All of the children were there; a white vehicle kept passing by the harbor. For some reason they thought that it was law enforcement and that the end was near. They thought they were going to be taken away. So they all talked amongst themselves: she, Rosie, Kiani, Elizabeth and Serafino—they knew they had to take care of themselves and commit suicide. They each wrote a suicide letter. In the letters they each had to deny it was Marcus's idea, and claim it to be their own. There was a bag with several guns. Sofia grabbed a gun and bullets, looked at it, and realized she had no idea what to do or how to use the gun. She remembers sending one of the children ashore, who somehow made contact with Marcus who told them not to do anything. Sofia sat and waited. When one of the children arrived back to tell the news, she remembered being so happy that they didn't have to kill themselves. At the time, she was about 11 years old, the same age as Serafino. Elizabeth, Jr. was around 9 years old—all of these young minds were taught by Marcus how to proceed with the suicide mission. Sofia was familiar with the .22 caliber handgun Marcus had because she was with him when he bought the weapon at a place off of Shield and Blackstone streets in Fresno, Ca; she said the shop is no longer there.

It was at around age 12 where experiences for Sofia began to grow gruesomely strange…Marcus began to touch her at least once a month; his hands to her breast and her vagina which he would often rub. To offset the strangeness of this feeling, Marcus would tell Sofia that he was simply preparing her for the husband who she would one day give the ultimate pleasure. At age 13, Marcus taught her how to perform oral sex on him until the point of arousal, at which they would then have sex. Sofia explained that she did not know at the time that such acts were wrong.

By age 15 or 16 years of age, Sofia was asked by Marcus to do strip moves; she would dance around him and it would arouse him. To satisfy him, she would orally copulate him. She recalled one occasion where Marcus asked her if he could stick a Primatene asthma bottle in her vagina—she agreed.

Around age 17, Sofia described an incident where she would suck on Marcus's nipples or kiss him while he was having sexual intercourse with her sister Ruby, who was two years younger than her. When asked to perform sexually with all of her sisters and cousins, Sofia at first refused. Through manipulative calming words, Marcus eventually worked on her, telling her how they only loved each other, and that it was just them. Eventually Sofia was forced to orally copulated either her sister Ruby or her cousin Sebhrenah, while the other watched.

If the girls refused to have sex, they would be punished emotionally, according to Sofia, who continued her testimony to Ochoa. Marcus would either refuse to talk to her, or make derogatory comments about her body, and compare it to Kiani's or one of the other girls and make her feel bad. He would also become verbally abusive.

After the sexual encounter, Marcus would make sure this sexual conduct was what they wanted. He would ask them for their consent after the encounter.

Although the preliminary testimony stated that Sofia said she would orally copulate Marcus and then have sex, it is not defined as sexual intercourse. When directly asked when she began having physical sex with Marcus—intercourse—it was noted that such activity started at age 18 for Sofia. It was then she remembered the references to David Koresh, a cult leader of the Branch Davidian tribe in Waco, TX, discussed in a later chapter. Sofia recalls the suicide mission that occurred with Koresh and the many wives he had at the time. Marcus would make many statements in regard to Koresh being for God and that the state was going to come in and take away the children, according to Sofia. Marcus believed all of Koresh's children would be going to Heaven. Marcus would frequently talk about Koresh to the girls, about his beliefs and ways. In fact, whenever there was something on the television about Koresh, Sofia and the other girls were brought in and asked to watch it; this did not include the boys.

At one point, Sofia explained that Marcus wanted to have more children for the Lord; he asked the girls to have children with him in the name of the Lord. He asked if they would be willing to be surrogate mothers for Elizabeth and himself. For her these everyday teachings began at age 16. Marcus would pound into their heads that the world was ending, Jesus is coming, the end is near; and before you go to Heaven, it's a woman's duty to have children for the Lord.

On the contrary, Elizabeth said her two nieces, Sofia and Ruby, were seductive towards her husband and offered on their own accord to have children for them; Elizabeth was initially unaware that it would be with her husband, Marcus, according to a brief conversation about this matter. Elizabeth also noted that Sofia was having many problems with her significant other at this time, and she would confide in Elizabeth and Marcus on what to do. She noted Sofia was very unhappy in this relationship and found solace in returning to the Wesson family.

The problems were just beginning for Sofia, who was then an 18 years-old working on a job at a restaurant; this created a whole host of other problems. One of her sisters, (female cousins) told on her that she was possibly talking to a young man. The children were all taught to tell on each other by Marcus, who wanted the girls to stay out of any serious relationship with boys. Sometimes Marcus would take all of the girls and meet with them to ask who was doing what with what boys. He would keep them there for hours until somebody cracked.

In Sofia's incident, she was laughing with her older male cousin Dorian, Marcus's oldest son; Marcus questioned her about this in detail and informed her that with any boy or man, "When you talk to them, you are touching his mind. You are making him think about sex." Sofia was spanked for the accusation of talking to Dorian seductively.

By age 23, Sofia was ready to move out and would not be allowed to take her son Johnathan. Marcus decided to drive her someplace, leaving the Santa Cruz harbor, heading towards San Jose. He began to ask her many questions along the way, especially if she was ready to confess her sins. Shortly, they began to drive back to the harbor and on the way, he parked the car and asked Sofia if she loved Jesus Christ. She replied, "Yes, I love Jesus Christ." The conversation then perpetuated to Marcus asking her again if she was ready to confess her sins; she said yes. He then asked her if she wanted to ask him for forgiveness for her sins and she replied yes. He swung a knife at her and missed. The second swing stabbed her in the right breast. She told him that she wasn't ready to die. He told her he thought she was ready since he had confessed her sins to him. They then walked into the boathouse and Marcus immediately told his wife, Elizabeth Wesson, who was in shock at what had happened. Elizabeth began to tend to her injury. Marcus having a nursing background also looked at it and told her she would be fine; Sofia never went to the hospital for the wound.

Thereafter Sofia was not allowed to leave the boat for anything, not even work. She was also not allowed to interact with the girls, nor her baby Johnathan, unless she was breastfeeding him. If the child attempted to come to her, he would get spanked and so would she.

Most members of the Wesson family deny that Sofia was ever stabbed and that she continually made up stories such as these to get attention. Serafino mentioned that his cousin, Sofia, was always in trouble, hanging around the wrong crowds, especially boys, and that's what caused her to be in trouble so much and away from the other siblings.

When acknowledging the treatment of her own son in the Wesson household, Sofia said that her baby cried a lot and Marcus beat him when he was four to six months old. Marcus had first warned her to discipline her own child. Sofia told him that she couldn't, since he was only four months old. He would make her get a small switch off a tree and wrap duct tape around it; she just couldn't bring herself to do it. She pleaded with her Aunt Elizabeth to stop him from beating her baby. She replied there was nothing she could do.

Ruby's Side

In Ruby's testimony, Sofia's sister, Marcus's niece, was interviewed by Officer Richard Glen Byrd, veteran of at least 13 ½ years on the police force. He stated in his testimony on April 8th that he interviewed her at a friend's house.

Born on November 7, 1977, Ruby came to live with the Wesson

family at the North College residence when she was seven or eight years old. She explained that her mother, Rosemary, gave her children, (including Rosie and Sofia) to Marcus Wesson to raise, except for the oldest boy.

Ruby also described how their lives changed in the same manner her sister Sofia did; they were home schooled, their style of dress changed similar to that of their cousins: long dresses with scarves over their heads. Ruby explained that Marcus said they had to do this because women weren't suppose to show their head to God, only a man could, and because women were considered secondary to men, they must keep their heads covered.

During the religious teachings, she explained that the boys were on one side, the girls were on the other; they had to be kept separated. The two-hour Bible study in the morning would include Marcus quoting and interpreting scripture. They were expected to sit quietly and listen, without falling asleep, or else they would be punished. If a child fell asleep during Bible study, Marcus would take that child to another room and administer spankings—usually 12—or beatings. Then the child would have to come back out and continue with prayer. The spankings would continue until that child stopped falling asleep during the lecture.

Ruby also confirmed that Marcus would call himself Christ, and the only way through the Father was by him; in order for them to go to heaven, they needed to believe in him.

The sexual activity started for Ruby as soon as she got there. She said she remembered when it started because another child was stillborn at that time. This upset Ruby and Marcus asked her why since she didn't even know the child. Nevertheless she cried so Marcus brought her that night into his bed. He rubbed her vagina over her clothing, until he eventually digitally penetrated her. Ruby began having sexual intercourse with Marcus at age 15; he would perform the "pull out" method so as not to get her pregnant before she turned 18.

Prior to that, she also described a time when she was forced to orally copulate Marcus, and times when he would have other siblings orally copulate her. Again she described another memory of continuous digital penetration session where Marcus would not stop until she would have an orgasm. Ruby would be upset, crying during the entire process.

There was another time when he asked her to bring Sofia with her into the room. Marcus took Sofia's shirt off and fondled her breast. He then took out his penis and forced her to orally copulate him. Ruby expressed that she started to gag and cough, enraging Marcus. He then demanded she swallow, but she didn't want to. Marcus told her, "Real women swallow," so she did.

When Ruby was 13, Marcus approached her and told her he wanted her as his wife. She was honored at the time, thinking this was normal. They married and the ceremony included just the two of them. Marcus brought in the Bible and they both placed their hands on it while reciting traditional wedding vows. She was now his wife, and she was to continue to do whatever he told her. If she didn't, she would not make it to heaven. He also told her she would be saved forever, as long as she was faithful to him, and that a wife could not refuse her husband. Anything done in the bedroom was not considered sinful. He would verify what he said with biblical passages, stating, "A woman who goes against her husband, that husband will start looking elsewhere."

During the interview, Ruby was hesitant and felt embarrassed. She would cry during the questioning, but was adamant about wanting to give the information.

As for what the girls had to do with each other, Ruby cried as she remembered Marcus asking her if she wanted one of the girls to give her oral sex. She told him she didn't want that. He then told her Rosie wanted to and that she was being greedy for not allowing her. Ruby gave in and allowed it to happen. As soon as the act began, Ruby closed her legs and faked an orgasm. Yet Marcus grabbed her thighs and squeezed them very hard, forcing her to open them. He then made the comment that she was selfish for not letting the sibling finish. She said Kiani performed oral sex on her as well and Marcus would get very angry with her if she said she didn't like it.

The act of having children with Marcus was twisted into an act of having children for God as well as for Marcus and his wife Elizabeth. Marcus told them to tell others who were outside of the household that they had been artificially impregnated; which was the big thing in the news during that time. There was also the other issue in Waco, TX that was creating big news that she remembers; David

Koresh. Every time something came on TV about Koresh, Marcus would get all charged and pumped up, and he'd gather all the girls around the TV and watch. He then would talk to them about what Koresh was doing for God. Her mother, Rosemary Solorio, would be upstairs watching television all day long. Whenever anything about Koresh came on, she would yell down stairs to Marcus, so he could gather the girls only.

Once a week Marcus would meet with the girls to make sure it was okay what he was doing to them sexually; he wanted to make sure if something were to happen that all the sexual activities were with their consent. He wanted to prevent them from saying it was against their will.

It was also noted that the girls and boys grew up in separate living quarters; when they were living on the bus, the boys would be in the back of the bus, girls in the front, or vice versa. They weren't allowed to interact or talk to each other at all. If they were caught talking to each other, the girls would be the ones to receive the harsh discipline, not the boys. In fact, there was an incident that occurred at Ruby's job while she was bussing tables. One of her sisters walked by while a busboy was asking her how many settings she needed for a table. At their once a week meetings with the girls, the sister brought up the incident; Marcus asked her if she thought Ruby was just being business-like, or was she trying to talk to this boy. The sibling replied that she thought it was just business. Marcus then told her, "No, if she's comfortable enough to answer him, she must be talking to him." Ruby was then punished.

Ruby got to a point where she didn't want to tell on her sister Sofia because Sofia was getting in trouble all the time. Marcus seemed crueler to Sofia and would use her as an example all the time. When Sofia would disagree with Marcus, which was often, he would beat her for seven days straight. If any of the girls did not remind Marcus that they had a beating due for that day, then she would get a beating for not reminding him. Ruby began to agree with anything Marcus asked her to do, so that she would not be treated like her sister, Sofia.

Finally, Ruby was 17 ½ years old when she became pregnant by Marcus; this was okay according to him, as long as the girls were 18 by the time the baby was born. During her pregnancy, he continued to have intercourse with her.

Before the children were born, when it was just her, her sister and her cousins she called sisters, Marcus told them they would need to be willing to take their own lives for God if the outside world were to try to come in. These were once a week teachings, according to Ruby. They would also need to take their own children's lives if the outside authorities would come for them.

The more Ruby began to get into the work force, the more Marcus became abusive to her, assuming she was always talking to guys. She started running away and eventually Ruby felt if she didn't, she would be killed. She left her daughter, Aviv, behind. In Marcus's eyes, the child did not belong to Ruby, forcing the children tp stay because they were God's children.

Ruby soon became worried about her safety. According to her, Marcus, when it was time for—or necessary—for the children "to go to God," his soldier, who at the time was her sister Rosie, was to go out and kill the family members who were on the outside; no longer in his household. The purpose of this killing was so the sheltered family members wouldn't be subject to the sins of the world, and would remain with Marcus.

While still living in the Wesson household and working outside the home, Ruby was required to give all her money to Marcus; neither Marcus or Elizabeth worked outside the home according to Ruby.

Upon asking Elizabeth personally about the money issue, she stated Marcus would take the girls' money to manage it and put it in accounts so they would have something for their future.

When Kiani became pregnant at 18, Ruby remembers the family having to move to the mountains and live in the motorhome bus. Marcus had told them they needed to move since some of the relatives were asking about the paternal father of the child. These relatives were not buying Marcus's artificial insemination story.

Brandy

Finally, there was the other niece: Brandy Sanchez, born November 15, 1978, who was the first one to leave the Wesson household. Officer Ochoa interviewed Brandy on March 15.

Brandy remembered being taken out of the school system in the second grade, for some unknown reason while living at the North College address and attending Lowell Elementary School. She also remembered being schooled by her older sister, Sofia, who was only nine years old. Brandy admitted up to this day, she is still illiterate.

According to Brandy, Marcus often referred to law enforcement as Satan, and Marcus was the only one who could give the signal for death.

Once again Koresh was brought up; Brandy said Marcus wanted their family to be more like Koresh and his followers because they followed the Lord. When they would see Koresh on the news, Marcus would find biblical verses to support Koresh's actions, and then follow with a lecture.

Brandy also recalled the long sermons by Marcus from the Bible, the New Testament or King James Version that would evolve into one to three hours sessions. She would become so tired during these long sermons that she learned how to fall asleep with her eyes open, to try to stay awake or to perceive that she was still awake listening.

Then there were the talks: these were the biblical verses Marcus used to teach and justify why Brandy and the other girls should have sex, as well as have children with him, said Brandy. Marcus also reinforced that their sexual favors would make them better wives for their husbands. He would test the girls on the information by asking them how hey felt, if they believed in what he was teaching, and she always felt compelled to answer yes. Brandy said she was so young then, she didn't know anything different.

Brandy also explained that she had been fondled since the age of eight; her vagina and breasts, just like the rest of the girls, every day, for years. Marcus taught her how to masturbate and orally copulate him when she was 11 years old. She even recalled a time when Marcus forcefully made her orally copulate for as long as she could go; one time she lasted an hour and a half.

By age 14 or 15, she started having sexual intercourse with Marcus. She was also made to have sexual relations with her own sisters and sometimes Marcus's daughter Sebhrenah.

In regard to his teachings, Marcus's main reason for not allowing the mothers to take their children out of the household would be so that he could keep them until they grew to the age of seven-years old; that would give him enough time to mold the child just like him, according to Brandy.

Finally Brandy had a way out of her sexually abusive situation; Marcus had impregnated Kiani, Sofia and Ruby, and he wanted to hide the pregnancies by moving to Santa Cruz. Brandy, just 17, ran away and never turned back.

Sofia's Credibility

In a cross examination of detective Ochoa by public defender Torres, it was found that Sofia never referred to the suicide mission as a pact, but as a religious belief. Via the police investigation, the suicide notes Sofia spoke of had not been found yet, forcing the defense to suggest that those statements spoken by Sofia were hearsay. The defense suggested there were no written teachings consistent with the suicide pact. It was also not clear whether Sofia believed in the second coming of the Christ, as well as Marcus referring to himself as the Christ. The police never questioned Sofia on this concept, the defense complained.

In regard to the severe beatings of the children that Sofia professed, the defense pointed out there were no severe bruises or, cuts, or evidence of strikes on the legs with some object, such as a switch, on the autopsy report. Such accusations and hearsays were questionable to the credibility of the witness. They even cited the People versus Dagget case where a child's testimony in regard to molestation; the knowledge can be attacked by knowledge of other conduct. It was possible, in their minds, that Sofia could have obtained information through the other alleged molests by her uncles. It was confirmed that Sofia was molested by her uncles and a brother before the age of nine.

As for Ruby, she said in the interview that she was married to Marcus at 13, but didn't start having intercourse with him until age 15. The defense saw this as very inconsistent. Not only that, Police Bryd didn't ask for clarity in relation to the information that Ruby was married for two years prior to having sexual contact with Marcus.

Kiani's Truth

Saved by the preliminary hearing where Detective Douglas Reese had interviewed Kiani Wesson, the suicide agreement and the sexual misconduct of Marcus Wesson was confirmed by Marcus's own daughter, Kiani, who loved him as a father and a husband. Maybe Sofia's childhood memories would be affirmed by her own cousin/sister, Kiani.

Her demeanor was very calm and matter of fact; Kiani told detective Reese she had sexual intercourse with Marcus and had kids with him. She was also well aware that Rosie, Ruby and Sebhrenah were having sexual intercourse with Marcus. She mentioned that her mother, Elizabeth, could no longer have babies, so they each wanted to give one to her. They were going to be surrogate mothers for her. However, they were instructed to tell relatives they went to a sperm bank since there was already hate within the Wesson family.

Kiani continued to state that Marcus did not work outside the home, but the sisters did; they would earn money and Marcus would manage it for them.

The questionable suicide pact was true: Kiani said the girls were instructed to shoot the kids if anyone ever came to take them. She believed it was Marcus's idea; Marcus told Kiani that the government was not to take her children away. If they ever did come and attempt to take the children, the family was supposed to give up their lives and go up to God, rather than let the government have them. The goal was not to have the children taken to different parts of the world like some other children; which Marcus told them would happen. The key difference in each of the women's testimony is the timing: Kiani said the suicide pact was discussed briefly, some five years earlier from March 12th; whereas Sofia, said this was something brought up often.

When she was 19, Kiani married Marcus in a private ceremony. With the Bible, they exchanged vows only between them. However, Marcus performed the same ceremony with Sofia, Sebhrenah and Ruby, according to Kiani.

Marcus first began to touch his daughter Kiani at the young age of eight. Once a month, or so, he would kiss her on the lips, neck and rub her body and chest area with her clothes on, eventually rubbing and caressing her vagina. Also, Kiani did say that their father officially asked them to have babies, and if it would be okay.

The girls were free to leave at any time from the households, according to Kiani, but they would have to leave the children there with her father and mother Elizabeth.

To conclude detective Reese's interview with Kiani, the most intriguing statement from her thereafter was that she was sad about losing her two children, but knows that if they (the government) was going to take them, she'd rather see them go to God rather than go to the CHP. Let it be noted, this statement made by Kiani was later clarified by Detective Reese to mean CPS, (Child Protective Services).

Jurisdiction Problems

In the charges of these sexual counts against Marcus Wesson, public defender Jones reiterated that the jurisdiction for some of these charges were questionable and inaccurate, "Most of these charges are vague to age," said Jones in a closing argument of the preliminary hearing.

"…I think there was some evidence that when they were—they lived at North College when I think it was Brandy was seven years old. That was 1985, I believe. And none of these charges involved 1985(referring to the March 12th case.) It's later on. And I don't believe the prosecution had pinned down to the satisfaction of the required level of evidence the whereabouts of this family at the times in question."

However Prosecuting Attorney Lisa Gamoian's approach was more about the sexual victims not having free will because they were conditioned in a certain way for many years, not just during one instance of time.

"According to his (Marcus's) teachings, over the course of many, many years was—was grooming sexual assault victims; and in fact, Kiani Wesson still believes it's okay to have sex and children with her own father. That's how good of a teacher Mr. Wesson is. That's how effective his teachings were and still remain."

Rebellious Daughter

Gypsy

Then there was 19 year-old Gypsy Wesson, a younger daughter of Marcus and Elizabeth. Detective Reese found in the interview she too was sexually touched by her father around six or seven years old, once a month, in the same manner as her sister Kiani. It would be Officer Leal that would interview her March 14th—two days after the tragedy—at around 3:30 PM at the Street Violence Bureau Office in Fresno.

Gypsy was not living with the Wesson family when this incident occurred but could describe her growing with a controlling and strict father, known to be Marcus Wesson. She said they were not allowed to socialize with others outside the immediate family, nor were they allowed to have friends.

She also confirmed that they studied the King James Version of the Bible at least twice a day, in the morning and afternoon. They also received an hour sermon by Mr. Wesson every day. The children had to follow the strict rules of the house or else be subjected to punishments, which included week long spankings or counseling. For a serious violation, such as one of the daughters, cousins from the family, or the brothers or cousins fist fighting among themselves or not listening to her dad, or denying him, Gypsy said they would be spanked once in the morning and once in the evening prior to going to bed. No one would defy her father.

Bringing up the suicide discussion, Gypsy said Marcus started talking about this around 1995. Ironically, against her sister Kiani, Gypsy's testimony matched Sofia's in regard to the frequency of the talk; the suicide discussions were everyday. They (the Wesson family) were afraid that the outside world would influence the small children, and if the CPS or law enforcement were to attempt to break up the family they had a plan: the older adults or older teenagers were to kill the children off, the smaller ones, and they were all to commit suicide. Gypsy said that Marcus was the giver of this idea, but never instructed anyone on how to carry out the plan. All of the children knew Marcus had a firearm but he didn't teach anyone how to use it, according to Gypsy. Gypsy, quoting her father, said daily he would ask them, "If the time came, would you be ready?" This meant they would have to carry out the suicide plan when the time came; when police arrived to break up the family to end their lives.

Timid and reluctant, Gypsy did not want to talk about the sexual-related incidents and was very closed about making any statements; she told officer Leal she was just five years-old when her father, Marcus, started touching her inappropriately one or twice week, underneath her clothing. Gypsy said she knew the difference between good and bad touch: she knew that a bad touch meant sexual, against her will. When explained to her that good touching meant a brother giving her a hug, she explained that she very much understood the difference and that her father would often kiss them in the mouth; like a husband and wife kiss.

To justify the molestations, Marcus would tell her and the other girls that he was getting them ready for their husbands, so they would know how to please them. Gypsy said that her father was doing a bad touch to all of the girls in the household; she had seen it done to them with her own eyes. During the molestations, the boys would be in one room and the girls in the other.

Before the molestation, Gypsy said he would ask her, "If you don't want me to touch you, I won't touch you." She said she always went along with it because she didn't want the others to look at her differently and for Marcus to treat her mean for no apparent reason. All of these happenings occurred at the house on 367 North College St., at Gypsy's Aunt Rosemary Solorio's home. She also said there other residences they lived at; two separate places on Cambridge. The last residence she did not have the address for, but they lived in a converted pool room in the back.

While living in the home, Gypsy said the only choice she had was to live their lifestyle or else... in July of 2003, she ran away from the home. Working at the Radisson Hotel in Fresno off of Van Ness, one of her brothers showed up to her job and told her Marcus was outside waiting in the car, and he really wanted to speak to her. She went outside and spoke to him, where he convinced her to go to their new residence at 761 Hammond. There he talked to her in depth.

He asked her to come back to the family, but she refused. When asked by him, "Are you still ready to die for the Lord" she said no. Admonishing Marcus about this suicide agreement, Gypsy told him that he had no right to choose the time when the children had to die because they had no way of making their own choices. They were children and she should not—and Marcus should not—be so controlling over people's lives. Marcus was upset because no one had ever talked back to him like she did. She then simply left the residence.

There was something odder than the alleged molestations stated by Gypsy; the testimony never reached the defense before the hearing that day, the defense was immediately shocked to hear it as they went along; the prosecution's due process was not being followed according to procedure.

Clearing up the Adventist Relation

Perhaps Marcus mixed his own tastes and views of his religion according to his conscience, which he most likely followed. Nevertheless, his religious views should not be confused with any religion relating to the Rastafarians or the Seventh Day Adventists. What should be honored is his mental state of mind and being, which surpassed his mental judgment and conscience, leading him astray. We delve into psychological existence of Marcus Wesson and his family later in chapter nine.

It is well known that the Adventist groups believe the second advent or coming of Christ was to be about a thousand years later, around the millennium. It is said they believe Jesus wants his followers to refrain form alcoholic drinks, from the use of tobacco, and from the eating of pork. Professed in this religion is, "Get right with God, for the end of the world can come at any moment." According to author Bach, Adventist founder William Miller, born in Pittsfield, Massachusetts in 1782, did military service in the War of 1812 and came out of it so shaken because of the brutality and suffering he had seen, that at first he became an atheist, feeling there was no hope. Soon he was converted into a Baptist at a revival service at age 34 and then he was inspired by reading about the life of Jesus and his promise to return a second time. This prompted him to become a preacher and start a group based on his prediction of the second coming. They were known as the Millerites. Although his prediction of the second coming and the end of the world never came through, he left more than that in his death to more than 13 million people worldwide— Adventism. Known for their holy living, simple faith, and benevolent giving, Adventist celebrate Saturday as their Sabbath, follow a selfless ethic and yet are still strange and curious in the eyes of many who do not understand their faith. One thing to be known, according to author Bach, is that they see death as an unconscious sleep; that all men, good and evil alike, remain in the grave until the resurrection; that the resurrection of the just will take place as the second advent of Christ; and the judgment of the unjust will take place a thousand years later, at the close of the millennium.

Similar to the Adventist are the Jehovah's Witnesses' who are more vocal in their approach, going door-to-door to tell people of the last days and to get onboard with their organization to be saved.

May it be known that in today's world, all religions may seem estrange to one another; yet, they still uphold the presence of an Omnipresence that is Divine and a factor in their beliefs. To judge one from the other would be ridiculous and a waist of time. However information is the best way to rid ignorance. Below are questions and statements from the Central California Conference of Seventh-day Adventists in regard to the Marcus Wesson case.

1. What is the Seventh-day Adventist Church's reaction to the events in Fresno?

We share with all of Fresno a deep sense of anguish over the tragic events of this past Friday. At this time of tragedy, we pray that God will comfort those who have been hurt deeply by these senseless events.

2. Why is the Seventh-day Adventist Church releasing information now?

We have learned this information only since the tragic events of Friday. We had to search records looking for any information about Mr. Wesson. There are no records in any church about Mr. Wesson, but he did apparently have occasional sporadic contact with Adventist churches.

3. Is Marcus Wesson a Seventh-day Adventist?

As far as we can determine, Marcus Wesson has never been a member of any Seventh-day Adventist Church. Marcus Wesson has had sporadic contact with Adventist churches. His parents were members of a Seventh-day Adventist Church. As a child, he attended church   services with his parents. As an adult, he occasionally took some of his children to church services. He has attended the Central California Adventist Camp Meeting in Soquel a few times, once as recently as five or six years ago. Camp Meeting is a 10-day spiritual retreat held annually in late July. He was employed as a janitor at the Soquel campgrounds during camp meeting in the late 1980s and early 1990s. As Police Chief Jerry Dyer said on Monday, "This is not about religion... Seventh-day Adventists are good people."

4. Were any of the victims Seventh-day Adventists?

Yes. Sebhrenah Wesson joined the Fresno Hispanic Seventh-day Adventist Church in 1999. --Church members do not recall her, because she rarely if ever attended.

5. Were any other members of the extended family Seventh-day Adventists?

Yes. Kiana Wesson, Sofina Solorio, and Ruby Sanchez also joined the Fresno Hispanic Seventh-day Adventist Church in 1999. Church members don't recall these women either, saying they rarely if ever attended church services. Sofina Solorio is now a member and attending regularly an Adventist Church in the Bay Area. She joined in November 2003.

6. What is the Seventh-day Adventist Church's role for these family members?

The role of the church is to mourn with those who mourn. We are grateful to be able to minister to surviving family members who have suffered such immense loss. People turn to something outside themselves when they experience great tragedy, and often seek churches to help them in times of great grief. As Blaise Pascal said, "There is a God-shaped vacuum in every person." Times of crisis lead us to turn to God for solace. We count it a privilege to be able to serve people in difficult times.

7. Does the Adventist Church believe

No. Like all Christian churches, the Adventist Church finds murder, incest, and polygamy to be reprehensible.

8. Just what is the Adventist Church?

The Adventist Church is a mainstream Protestant church with more than 13 million members worldwide. We have churches, along with hospitals and schools, in more than 200 countries.

9. What does the Adventist Church believe?

We hold most beliefs in common with other Christian churches, including belief in Jesus Christ as God's divine son and our savior. We also have some distinctive beliefs that differ from other Christian churches.

As our name indicates, we worship on the seventh day of the week— Saturday— and we believe that Jesus is coming again soon.

In hopes that the above information brings understanding, we certainly appreciate these statements provided by the Adventist community who has been known to be truly thoughtful at heart and very giving and nourishing to all citizens.

How much can religion really influence a person's life? Apparently, it affects people's moral values and judgments in difficult situations that encumber their lives, determining hard, finite choices. Unfortunately, anything amoral becomes justified by those same religious values, often clouding the picture of right from wrong. It was inevitable that the Wesson family based all of their beliefs and daily rituals on religious principles, mostly influenced by Marcus. Some would believe this as dedication to one's faith; others, dedication to one's cult; a relative topic to extreme religion examined in the next chapter.

If a man would follow, today, the teachings of the Old Testament, he would be a criminal. If he would follow strictly the teachings of the New, he would be insane.
~Robert G. Ingersoll

"Woe to the worthless shepherd, who deserts the flock!
May the sword strike his arm and his right eye!
May his arm be completely withered, his right eye
totally blinded!"

~Zechariah 11:17; *The Bible*
(New International Version)

Revelation 6

Cult Ideals: The David Koresh Connection

"It is not a crime to belong to a cult"; stated Dr. Eric Hickey in his book, *Serial Murderers and Their Victims.* "The term means 'a system of religious worship; devotion or homage to a person or thing.' Nor is it a crime to practice beliefs of the occult—things that are 'kept secret, esoteric, mysterious, beyond the range of ordinary knowledge; involving the supernatural, mystical, magical'—provided those practices occur within an accepted legal framework."

Although such a term traditionally applied to the "notions of evil and demonology," as stated by Dr. Hickey, the term often refers to religious sects that are more securely segmented in one area of thought that is worshiped. These cults are designed by makers that create their own set of values and beliefs that are adopted or borrowed from other historically established religions. In this definition of a cult, most religions came from their own sects, expanding their membership; therefore, bringing about a more common belief system among other like minds. This would also explain one of the reasons why we have so many different religions today under the broad term "Christianity": which includes the Baptist, Jehovah's Witnesses, Seventh Day Adventist, Protestant, Methodist/Wesleyan, Lutheran, Presbyterian, Pentecostal/Charismatic, Episcopalian/Anglican, Mormons—all of these groups are relative in their beliefs about Jesus Christ, differing mostly by their own interpretations of his gospel and holy practices. Within some of these denominations, further segmentation exists. For instance, the Baptist denomination has the

Free Will Baptists, General Baptists, Separate Baptists and United Baptists. These fragmentations occur because of disagreements on beliefs and interpretations of the Bible, the concept of God, and what are acceptable and unacceptable moral behaviors.

From the Seventh Day Adventist denomination, another sect was born: Marcus Wesson's sect, which he modeled after the *Branch Davidians'*.

According to author B.A. Robinson, who wrote the article on the Ontario Consultants on Religious Tolerance website, the Branch Davidians was a splinter of the Seventh-Day Adventist (SDA) created by Victor Houteff, who had joined the SDA church in 1919. His beliefs deviated from main-line church doctrine. This became obvious when he wrote his book *The Shepherd's Rod* in which he outlined errors that he found within the church. He left the church and formed a new sect in 1929 called the *Davidian Seventh-day Adventists*. This group split further and eventually led to the organization of the *Students of the Seven Seals*, popularly known as the *Branch Davidians* (BD). In 1993, after a long standoff with the FBI, the Branch Davidian's compound burned down to the ground with a catastrophic outcome, where many individuals lost their lives. David Koresh, the leader of the Branch Davidian, led his followers to their destruction.

In 1981, Vernon Howell (1959-1993) joined the BD group as a handyman. In 1984, he married 14 year-old Rachel Jones, the daughter of a prominent member of the BD community. Soon after, Howell took over as the leader of the BD group in Waco, TX at Mt. Carmel. In 1990, Howell changed his name to David (after King David of the Israelites) Koresh (after the Babylonian King Cyrus). In 1992, Koresh renamed Mt. Carmel *"Ranch Apocalypse"* because of his belief that the final encompassing battle of Armageddon mentioned in the Bible would start at the BD compound.

Koresh established an international recruitment drive in 1985. According to author Robinson, the recruitment drive was aimed at SDA members (particularly those who had been excommunicated from the church due to their beliefs). This effort brought in members from Australia, Canada, Great Britain, etc. A number of businesses were created within the compound such as purchasing guns wholesale and legally reselling them at gun shows. At the time of the BD demise, (spring of 1993), there were 130 members living in Waco, TX. These members were multi-racial, multi-ethnic group of whom 45 of them were African-Americans.

According to Robinson, the BD's church beliefs were as follows:

• God has provided a prophet whose pronouncements are to be regarded on a par with the Bible.
• Christ's death on the cross provided salvation only for those who died before 32 CE. People who have died since will only be saved through the activities of the current BD prophet.
• They believe that the "lamb" mentioned in Revelation 5:2 is not Jesus Christ (as essentially all Christians believe) but is David Koresh himself. The lamb is to open up the seven seals and trigger the sequence which ends the world as we know it. This belief caused a great deal of misunderstanding; many Christians believe that Koresh viewed himself as Jesus Christ, and was thus psychotic.
• After the breaking of the seals, Christ would return to earth. A battle would occur in which the BDs would play a major role. The BD members alone would ascend to heaven to be with God.
• Massive confusion developed within the BD during the standoff. Koresh apparently believed that the BATF raid was in some way related to the Book of Revelation's Apocalypse and the war of Armageddon. However details did not fit. Koresh taught that it would occur in Jerusalem in 1995, not in Texas during 1993

In regards to the practices the church followed, they were questionable:

• The BDs at Waco led a communal, highly regulated and disciplined life: raising early, eating together, growing their own food, committing long intervals of time to Bible study, etc. Some members had jobs outside the community which contributed financially to the organization.

• They published a periodical "Shekineth Magazine"

• They held conventions which were synchronized with the Jewish feast days defined in Leviticus 23:4-43.

• Following Koresh's "New Light" doctrine, he began to persuade married women within the group to join him as "spiritual wives." This involved sexual access. Couples were separated and their marriages dissolved. All but Koresh and his spiritual wives were required to remain celibate.

• There were rumors that Koresh was sexually and/ or physically assaulting children in the community. Other rumors suggested that he had several "wives" who were in their mid teens. This was supported by statements from disgruntled ex-cult members and by a father involved in a custody suite. Strong physical punishment was used in the compound for discipline of children. There are allegations that infants as young as eight months were beaten with a paddle. However assertions of actual sexual abuse of young children are of unknown validity. Several investigations were conducted by local Child Protective Services; they turned up no evidence of sufficient quantity or quality to justify a charge. None of the children who left the compound during the siege exhibited any signs of abuse. However Koresh did state in a videotape that he is the father of more than a dozen children with several "wives" who he allegedly impregnated at the age of 12 or 13. If he was telling the truth, then he certainly was guilty of statutory rape. During the standoff, the physical and sanitary conditions in the compound had seriously degenerated. The U.S. Justice Department reported that "It was unhealthy at best, and potentially life-threatening at worst, for children to continue, to be forced to live in such an environment." 1

• They assembled large supplies of arms; one source estimated 11 tons of arms including antitank rifles.

• During the 1990's, all but one of the elements which

are commonly found in doomsday cults were present at Ranch Apocalypse. Only one element that has been generally found in other destructive cults was missing. There does not appear to have been strict control of information in to the compound.

Like Houteff and Koresh, who believed that they were messengers sent by God to administer spiritual cleansing of the chosen ones, Marcus Wesson became the spiritual leader for his family, and taught them what he believed to be spiritual cleansing doctrine to his family. Furthermore, according to court transcripts and testimony by family members, Marcus would threaten his family members if they tried to leave, and for those who left the family, they were considered tainted individuals who were infected with worldly sins that could harm the rest of the group if they came into contact with the non-sinners. Therefore, the family members that decided to leave had to be taken care of—terminated for the safety of the rest of family members.

The end-of-the-world phenomena or Armageddon was another belief that Wesson shared with Koresh. According to author Robinson, the BD observed the approaching 76 heavily armed employees of the Bureau of Alcohol Tobacco and Firearms (ATF), and interpreted the approaching ATF employees as the Apocalypse and the Battle of Armageddon, which they so devoutly had been studying and anticipating for years, was finally becoming a reality in their very own eyes. For Wesson, the end meant the law enforcement or the Child Protective Service intervening in their lives. He did not want his family to dissipate because this meant the end for him. In a delusion that the end was near, Marcus would go to desperate measures, allowing his own children to be killed at point blank range. He would be reassured that all of his children would be safe in heaven.

Other uncanny similarities between Koresh and Wesson include the practice of marrying underage girls. Koresh admitted having wives and fathering children with girls as young as 12 years old; Marcus Wesson followed a similar practice, too. He married his main wife Elizabeth when she was only 15 years old, and had relationships with his daughters and nieces while stressing the values, beliefs and practices of Koresh. They were all teenagers as well, when he self-married them to him. According to the preliminary hearing, Wesson's children stated that their father admired Koresh, was fond of Koresh's work, and saw Koresh's religious rite as a justification and affirmation of his own teachings and religious practices.

The Role of Women

Evaluating the women would require deeper understanding of their world. In a personal interview, Dr. Eric Hickey explained, "It's interesting, people who fall into cults like that. They are so easily controlled...Those incestual groups like this are doomed for destruction because they are creating people who have all kinds of mental, emotional, physical defects. He (Marcus) wanted to keep the bloodline pure. (He wanted to keep it all in the family) So, that's child abuse; it's incest, sodomy—and yeah, she (Elizabeth) knew all and saw all of her daughters get pregnant. She knew her daughters were not promiscuous."

The women, out of love for their father, leader and master, would follow what Christ wanted them to do, which meant for them to be obedient, respectful and to not question whatever their father asked them to do. Of course, the daughters and nieces wanted to be good in the eyes of Marcus, even if it meant for them to behave as his wives. The misconception was that whatever would better the cause under the name of religion is right; there was no wrong, no matter how deviant the act might have been. In the Wesson household, the children were seen as "Children of God." The daughters and nieces accepted the artificial insemination theory given to them because the children that they were bearing were for a higher cause.

What was defying and misleading in their belief system was the graphic sexual duties that the Wesson women were subjugated to perform, which was mixed with the ideologies of love for one's sibling, love for one's father and love for God. It is one thing to love one's father and God, but the love that Marcus propagated was something beyond the boundaries of normal love between a child and a parent. The conflicting ideas weighed heavily in some of the

Wesson women's' minds, and some of them could not handle such confusing ideology and ran away.

As we change our focus, may it be readjusted with our eyes; the most revealing thing would be the mystery of the eye shootings: they indeed do tell all. In the afterlife, they have long been considered a gate to heaven or a gate to hell, according to the next chapter.

The more I study religions the more I am convinced
that man never worshipped anything but himself.
~Richard Burton

"Woe to the worthless shepherd, who deserts the flock!
May the sword strike his arm and his right eye!
May his arm be completely withered, his right eye
totally blinded!"

~Zechariah 11:17; *The Bible*
(New International Version)

Revelation 7

Eyes That Tell All

The eyes; known as the window to the soul, have confounded man for centuries. Men and women have fought, just from an evil look of the eye. Sight is an impressionable gift that could be one's blessing or one's curse.

In the case of the Wesson family, it was their curse; eight victims all shot in the right eye... someone would see this as the most puzzling part of the case; the mystery confined within another mystery. However the code can be deciphered according to the religious definitions that Marcus controlled his environment, himself and his family. Since religion was a high priority, all of the way around, without any room for change, then it must be understood that nothing was compromised, not even the simplest notion of all of the children being obedient because they were good sons and daughters; the obedience was much deeper and could be understood as respecting the religious rite that was imposed on them from an early age.

Historically, eyes have represented major facets of life, determined many emotions and represented powerful symbols. They eyes embody the personality of those who twinkle them in order to flirt with them or use them to "mean-mug" or for other reasons. others. The eyes can tell us if someone is a little off centered mentally, disturbed or depressed. Even on the back of our American *dollar*, a wide, shinning eye is housed within a pyramid, representing the all-seeing power of our nation, (The Right Eye of Horus, adopted from the Ancient Kemetic Egyptian culture.) It is this same bodily appendage that can wrongly inform of us of what we see; hide us from what we are not ready to see, protecting our brain from rationale that could hurt our sensitive ego. The eyes let us develop our own reality around us, they watch out for danger or often overlook it, depending what we are able to cope with during that moment in our lives. In the book *Metu Neter Volume 2*, the author Anuk Ausar stated, "Visual perception and thinking is the key to unification of our consciousness and ourselves with the world." He continued, "It is well known that to be able to look squarely in the eye of an opponent required and invoked courage, which is felt as a rise in temperature." This fact would only demonstrate the unique power of our eyes that control emotions, actions and even our demeanor.

It is also known the left and right eye represent very different parts of our brains: the *right eye* is controlled by the left, male oriented side of the brain which represents numbers, letters, reasoning, the creation of sentences and thoughts relative to concrete facts and processing language. The *left eye* is controlled by the right, female oriented side of the brain and represents the subtle influences of intuition, aesthetic reasoning, art, nuance, metaphor, color, music appreciation and the instinct of the female. All of the children— but one—were shot in their right eyes; the worldly left brain of consciousness and rationale. This is the side that helps us function in a world that uses mostly logic to explain everything. This would be the eye not needed in heaven, perhaps. One theory includes that this eye would block the deceased victims from entering the heavens as ghosts, stuck to the logics of this world, wanting a rationale to their deaths. Thus the shooting in the right eye would free them of the connection of this thought; all worldly pasts and memories would dissipate, allowing the souls to start anew—it is possible that the very bright and intelligent Marcus Wesson perceived this idea when mastering his finite religious beliefs. Author Ausar stated, "The evil, being the domination of Man's life by the left hemisphere, (right eye) which hears the world, i.e., lives in darkness, because it cannot see.

The good and the salvation comes through the right hemisphere (left eye) which is our function of seeing, understanding, and unification." Ausar said that according to the ancient Egyptians, the left eye, which governs understanding and spirituality, is the symbol of the omniscience and omnipresence of god. In the book, Dictionary of Symbols, authors Jean Chevalier and Alain Gheerbrant explained that in ancient times, the right eye represented the sun, the left eye the moon. The two eyes together present a dualistic vision, which is also a form of mental perception. They continued by taking from the writings of Angelus Silesius who wrote, "The Soul has two eyes: one is fixed on time, the other on eternity." And still another great philosopher continued that one eye represented love, the other the rational function—correlating with the shooting deaths of the children who came from a sanctimonious religious background.

Although these are all theories I surmised from research and by analyzing the religious intent of Marcus Wesson, one fact still remains; the child of Sebhrenah, Marshey St. Christopher Wesson, was shot in the left eye—the spiritual pathway of love and to God. What would this symbolize the one soul left behind to help solve the family mystery? It almost sounds convenient or a little disturbing to consider this a possibility—a soul in purgatory (something Marcus and his family did believe.) Or, maybe it was just the nervous twitch of Sebhrenah's finger on the trigger that slipped; in her hysterical state, she may not have realized that her own child's eye was shot in the left until the deed was done. Subconsciously it is said we all do what we are suppose to do, or at least what we desire to do; could it be possible that this would not be a mistake?

The shooting of the eye as a whole can also be attributed to Marcus's extensive military and medical training; most assuredly he knew that behind both eyes stood the brain, a quicker death and shock to the consciousness of the children who would die immediately from such wounds instead of suffering in pain.

According to Dr. Hickey, the above theory could be true, "the eye to him (Marcus) represents the lights to the soul. It may have been that he knew that shooting to the eye was a definite death shot.

Maybe something religious, you know these cult things, it could have been if they were all shot the same way—I have no idea.

Dr. Hickey suggests that there was a pattern there, "If he had a reason for doing that I suspect that it was some kind of control issue, (he knew they would inevitably die this way) see some people get shot in the head and it doesn't kill them.

To explain why the children never struggled as they watched others being shot in the eye, Dr. Hickey said, "They may not have known that they were going to be shot in the eye. And they may have done them (the children) one at a time. See they may have worked together, too, his daughter, and they may have taken one at a time in the room and not told them and just said, 'Okay, I want you to look over this way,' and then boom—not told them. And most of them were young, so they wouldn't be suspecting, they wouldn't have a clue: six, seven, five years-old, three years-old, they're not going to know, they are the easy ones. So it was just the older ones; I mean how many were older, a couple of them? He could droop a couple of them and the rest he could put hem all in one room, they might stand there and cry but they wouldn't know—these are defenseless children."

If time should reveal the logic on this matter, a better understanding will help the public know the power of the unknown that is beyond our visual perception of this earth.

The power is not left in the eyes, it is also instilled in the hair, according to the next revelation to follow that helps us understand why Marcus is not willing to cut his dreadlocks, as others have suggested.

> *But shapes that come not at an earthly call, will not depart*
> *when mortal voices bid.*
> ~William Wordworth

"The hoary head is a crown of glory, if it be found in the way of righteousness."

~Proverbs 17:31; *The Bible*

Revelation 8

Dreadlocks and Pig Tails

Dreadful, dreaded, **"dreadlocks"**; the word almost sounds like a conspiracy that warps the Western mind and conjures up images of pot-smoking Rastafarians; therefore, mystifying even more the look of the adorned.

Ironically, the lock, itself, is similar to that of a microscopic pig tail, twisted or curled so tightly, giving it the appearance of matted hair.

Yet still the looks, stares and questions arise when the public eyes veer at those who have them.

Marcus Wesson is certainly a dread-look considered extreme by many, creating irrational fears in the hairstyle itself. People often look at this man, noticing his long locks, matted with gray streaks that wildly style his head. It would be no wonder to have a misconception of such a hair style, laced with fear and the unknown.

I know of a black male with very long dreadlocks who ran a nonprofit community organization oriented around children in Fresno, Ca. One parent naively considered him to be connected with Wesson and stopped the child from going to the community facility. The dreadlocked gentleman was furious and offended to be questioned by the parent on whether he had affiliation with the accused mass murderer.

I, myself, as a wearer of locks have gone through my own oppositions within my culture; black people are still learning their natural roots that have been straightened with strong chemicals and hot combs, straying them away from matted hair; the abnormal.

People warned me not to get them for fear of public scrutiny and job security were excuses used in their reasoning. However, there must be some truth to such fears linked to economic standing because most professionals steer away from the hair choice of locks. Although the hairstyle harbors many common myths; in our society, it is still considered too "dreadful" to wear because of its look and reputation. Therefore the wearer must take all of these things into consideration—making a conscious decision—before putting such a permanent structure, way of life and a list of stereotypical ideals in the minds of others. Perceptions must be honored; one should not take a defensive stance against ignorance; a more understanding approach should suffice.

In a play I wrote, called, *Bench Memoirs*, I incorporated the struggles of young black girls and women with their hair, in hope that people would develop an understanding the tribulations black people have gone through historically with their hair—the entangled kinks are easier to understand once they are dramatized.

This chapter clears up the common myths of dreadlocks in relation to Marcus Wesson, who has had many remarks and looks of horror by the public who look at his dancing ropes of hair that swing past the bends of his knees.

"Dreadlock"—Word Origin

It is important to know that the term "dreadlocks" is not a universal term, although it is used as so in the American culture. Many other cultures have described such a hairstyle throughout history using a word of their own. Others often use the word interchangeably: "locks," versus "dreadlocks," which is not recommended. It is better to use the indigenous word, if not available then "locks" will do. Today the word "dread" is extended to various uses as an adjective, adverb, noun etc., not only denoting the hairstyle of a "dread."

The word originally came from the specific lifestyle of the Rastafarian. "Dreadlocks" is of Jamaican origin that sprouted from the early stages of the Rastafarian movement; people were afraid of the Rastamen (dread means "fear" or "horror").

However Knotty Vic Dicara, author of the essay "The History of Dreadlocks," stated in his essay that,

At the turn of the Twentieth Century, a socio-religious movement started in Harlem, NY by Marcus Garvey, found an enthusiastic following amongst the Black population of Jamaica. This eclectic group drew their influences from three primary sources (1) the Old and New Testaments, (2) African tribal culture, and (3) The Hindu culture that had recently become a pervasive cultural force in the West Indies.

The followers of this movement called themselves 'Dreads,' signifying that they had a dread, fear, or respect for God. Emulating Hindu and Nazarite holy men, these 'Dreads' grew matted locks of hair, which would become known to the world as 'Dreadlocks'— the hair-style of the Dreads.

Soon after, this group would focus their attention on the Ethiopian Emperor Ras Tafari, Haile Selassie, and thus became known as Rastafarians. But the term 'Dreadlocks' stuck.

Another explanation began to evolve from the aforementioned historical bounds of the word into something more spiritually qualifying: the locks bearer is the one who is the fearer, biblical fear of the Lord, that is. However through my research, I am inclined to believe that the latter explanation was created to fit today's word origin.

Perpetuated Dreadlock Myths and Wesson

After talking to Darling Burch, the correctional officer at the facility that holds Marcus Wesson, it is noted that she and all the other officers noticed an intolerable stench coming From Wesson's locks.

"…somebody asked me, 'well do he wash his hair?' If he do, it takes a long time to dry, and that may be why it smells so bad, you know, 'cause it's so thick and here he don't get no blow dryer, you know what I mean, so…when you wet all that stuff, it's thick, it's long, it's matted."

And in describing the smell she said, "They (the dreadlocks) smell like somebody who ain't bathed in years…um, something dead. I can't describe it but it's a terrible smell."

Unfortunately there are some wearers who perpetuate the myths of dreadlocks such as Wesson, in this case, because they aren't taken care of properly.

For the record, I have presented below common myths that are dispelled to help inform the public. Here are a few myths mentioned by the company, African By Nature, in an article, "Dreadlocks More than Just Fashion," by Editor Mad Theory in 2003, courtesy of urbanelements.net :

"All Dreadlocks are Dirty": This is probably the biggest myth about dreadlocks. One popular urban legend concerning this myth is that when Bob Marley died of cancer in 1981, the doctors found a few dozen new species of lice in his hair. This simply is not true. Far from being dirty savages, Africans have had methods of cleaning and caring for braids and dreadlocks for centuries. With today's modern science, even more ways exist to clean dreads with commercial soaps and solutions specifically designed for this style of hair.

"Dreadlocks are long, big and thick": An employers' biggest fear is that their employees will show up at work one day with the thick, loose, knotty dreads that Marley helped to popularize. What they fail to realize is that there are many different styles of dreads that can easily conform to almost any dress code. In fact, the most popular styles of dreads nowadays are the small, tight twists that can fit under most hats. All the employer needs to do is   specify the length (shoulder, middle of back, etc.) and the employee can be responsible for making sure that it looks professional.

"Anyone who wears dreadlocks smokes marijuana": It seems that some people associate dreads with weed smokers, probably because of the hairstyle's connection to Rastafarians   a n d their exaggerated connection to marijuana smoking. The truth is that wearing dreads has absolutely nothing to do with having an affinity for marijuana smoking. In fact, actual Rastafarians do not smoke marijuana recreationally. Pious Rastas only advocate smoking "ganja" as "wisdomweed," an aid to meditation and an "incense pleasing to the Lord." This aspect has been insanely sensationalized by the media, keeping Rastas and those who look similar to them stereotyped as drug selling and abusing criminals.

A couple more dreadlock myths are dispelled by NeAisha Campbell of Naturally NeAisha Enterprises at www.naani.com. She specializes in black hair and answered the following myths in a Q & A format of *De-Myth-ify Dreadlocks:*

"Dreadlocks have lice": The most common misconception about lice is that they only effect those with dirty hair. But in fact, lice are not discriminatory and are just as   comfortable on a clean head as they are a dirty one. So the overall condition of your hair does not make you more susceptible to being a louse host. These are parasitic critters who love warm, moist environments and feed off of your scalp. Because they can't live outside of these conditions more than 24 hours, so overall they really don't care whose head they rest on, just as long as they find a home.

You can probably spot a child with lice more quickly than an adult. Us grown folks know that it's not a good idea to scratch your head too vigorously, for too long in public. Kids on the other hand, when it itches, scratch it, if there's something up it, pick it. Either way, the bites from a louse cause the scalp to itch. The itching causes bacteria to be released which in turn cause the infected area to become inflamed.

To make a long story short, lice are not something that are attributable to dirty hair. Clean, dirty, it doesn't matter. Lice like to be able to be free to move about and prefer hair of shorter lengths. So, although they're not an impossibility, the very nature of dreadlocks decreases the chances that lice would survive on a dread host. More insulting is the idea that one could cohabitate with these critters for the lifetime of one's locks and bippity-bop around all day with no worries. I mean hell, what are we, Super Dread Folk who don't flinch when bit by blood sucking vermin?

Here's some basic info on lice.

How Lice Spread:

Their [lice] presence does not connote a lack of hygiene or sanitation practiced by their host. Head lice are mainly acquired by direct head-to-head contact with an infested person's hair, but may infrequently be transferred with shared combs, hats and other hair accessories. They may also remain on bedding or upholstered furniture for a brief period. Lice and their eggs are unable to burrow into the scalp. (Source: http://www.hsph.harvard.edu/headlice.html#what)

Lice and Black Folk:

African Americans are reported to have a much lower incidence of head lice than Caucasians, Hispanics, or Asian Americans. Pediatric Dermatology cites various studies that suggest the incidence among African American schoolchildren is less than half of one percent, while the incidence among their non-black schoolmates is usually more than ten percent.

Even though African Americans may be less susceptible to infestations, this should not, of course, be grounds for complacency; African Americans can and do get head lice."

"Dreadlocks Stink": This is the most popular and the most offensive of the dreadlock rumors. People who have never even been in the presence of dreadlocks hold this belief to be true. The myth was started because there is an overall belief in popular culture that in order to grow dreadlocks, one must refrain from shampooing his/her hair. For decades due to a lack of education and frequency of dreadlocks, there were some individuals who refrained from washing their hair and continued to perpetuate the myth. But in this day and age with the wealth of information that lay before us, there's no excuse for stinky dreads…So yes, unfortunately there are those individuals who still believe that in order to properly grow dreadlocks that they must refrain from shampooing their hair. They keep the myth alive and give us regular folks a bad name.

THE TRUTH: Dreadlocks don't stink. People who don't

shampoo their hair have stinky dreadlocks.

Wesson's hair power and the dreadlock history

The power is in the hair: when we think of the biblical Sampson and Goliath, we always remember the spiritual magic of Sampson's hair that disappeared once it was cut. The devastation and the feeling of insecurity, it can all be controlled by hair.

Think of the man in his mid-30's or earlier, balding; the familiar comb-over the bare spot technique, Rogaine, and any other miracle hair-growth products are sill used, no matter the cost. There are hair transplants that cost $4,000 or more…People will do anything for hair; it defines our appearance, who they are, and without it a person can feel undefined, lost, and even depressed or not as attractive.

Not only is hair an important part of a person's self-perception, it clearly defines one's presence, power and definition when entering a room. Throughout history dreadlocks have carried a stigma of power by the wearer, where he or she feels spiritually bound by his hair.

If we evaluate the common stereotype and belief of those who wear dreadlocks, we begin to decipher the misconceptions that unfold the matted truths. As a lock wearer, I have been questioned on whether I was a Rasta; this label puzzled me, stifling me from giving an appropriate answer as to why I wear dreadlocks. Then I realize I don't have to answer; it is a style of choice for some, spiritual significance for others.

Let's breakdown the Rasta rumor of those who sport this hairstyle by looking at the magazine article, "The History of Dreadlocks," from *The Rising Firefly Magazine*. Author Bouneith Inejnema Naba discusses the history of this rumor:

Dreadlocks have become so much associated with Rastafarian culture, which is, in turn, associated with smoking ganga, that few people know the real roots and history of dreadlocked hair. What are the traditional origins and meanings of dreadlocks?

New-generation Rastafarians will tell you that the culture of locked hair came, originally, from Africa, but any knowledge beyond the continent that locks came from is unknown. Where old-generation Rastafarians hold great pride in their natural hair and see it as a symbol of their fight against Babylon, non-violence, non-conformity, communalism and solidarity, and as a heavy spiritual statement, many new-generation Rastas see their dreads as a passport to smoking ganga and listening to Reggae music, not understanding the real Rastafarian culture and values. Where Rastafarians once shunned everything from Babylon, such as soda, alcohol and cigarettes, modern Rastas are often seen smoking, wearing designer clothing, eating meat and drinking beer. Wearing your hair naturally has become more of a status symbol than a spiritual decision, and people begin locking their hair so that they are seen as conscious, afrocentric, or different, rather than for honest spiritual and conscious reasons.

Where does Marcus Wesson exactly fit in? We know that he doesn't necessarily have to be Rastafarian and he does have strong roots in the Seventh Day Adventist teachings. His spiritual practices have always centered on staying pure, healthy and mindful; therefore, this surmounts to a person wishing to become closer to his god on his own spiritual precedent. I asked Elizabeth Wesson about this truth and indeed she confirmed that for spiritual and religious reasons, Marcus's long dreadlocks represent his spiritual power and guidance from God. Author Vic Dicara explained: "Dreadlocks, then, are universally symbolic of a spiritualist's understanding that vanity and physical appearances are unimportant. The counterpart to Dreadlocks is the shaven head, which has the same aim: disregard for vanity associated with physical appearances. Usually we find that spiritualists whose religious path includes elaborate rituals tend to embrace the shaven head technique as it affords a level of ritual cleanliness, while those mystics who adopt meditative or otherwise non-ritualistic paths prefer to disregard the air altogether and thus develop Dreadlocks."

How would one think such a concept? Again, if we look at history, we will find that dreadlocks were known for this exact purpose: spiritual profoundness and elevated consciousness in many cultures. According to Vic Dicara, dreadlocks have been historically represented throughout Christianity and Hinduism:

Dreadlocks are more than just a symbolic statement of disregard for physical appearance. Both Eastern and Western Traditions hold that bodily, mental and spiritual energies mainly exit the body through the top of the head and the hair. If the hair is knotted, they believe, the energy remains within the hair and the body, keeping a person more strong and healthy.

An excellent example from Western tradition is biblical Sampson, whose unsurpassed strength was lost when Delilah cut off his seven locks of hair. In classical India, all students on the spiritual path were directly enjoined by their scriptures to develop Dreadlocks as a means to detach them from physical vanity and aid them in the development of bodily strength and supernatural mental and spiritual powers.

Author Inejnema Naba also refers to historical figures in time who wore dreadlocks: "It is known that many Pharaohs had locked hair, and on Tutankhamen's mummy, dreadlocks can still be found intact... In the Bible, it states that those who don't shave, drink alcohol or eat meat are the closest to God; Jesus himself is shown with long hair!"

Swaying completely away from "physical vanity," according to former good friend Alex Garcia, it was known that Marcus Wesson was not a materialistic man. Alex described Wesson as usually dressed down in sweats and a dark colored t-shirt that hid the dirt and grime from him working all day.

"He wasn't into fashion at all," Alex explained, "that wasn't his thing. He would always have like a blue or black t-shirt; the clothes he wore, he wore a lot they would be more like dingy."

Alex continued to explain the spiritual path of Marcus, which was not a part of this physical world.

"He didn't care about material things, he didn't care about money, he just cared about his wife, his kids, eating healthy food, being happy and going to heaven; that's all he cared about. The guy could fix any stereo, any car, he could build any speaker—could you imagine a guy like that he could get a job anywhere. He could go to Radio Shack in a day, any minute to get a job there, (he could have gotten any job.) He really didn't like the hustle and bustle; I knew the guy for six years; never came home mad, never came home stressed out. He was just a calm guy; he always had the same tone of voice, the nice soft."

Alex further explained that Marcus at one time had a job as a banker that only lasted for six months or so because of the environment; Marcus was not fond of the sentiments of people and their attitudes. This would confirm Marcus's desired separation from the physical world: "He didn't like dealing with all that money and dealing with just that older crowd and the people that you deal with," Alex continued, " He said all that attitude, they (rude customers) would just have attitude, they were just mean and money hungry; he didn't like that. Then he just went back to his thing—wheeling and dealing. He just lived off of fruits and vegetables, that's all they lived off of."

I would almost confirm Marcus's need to express himself through nonconformity, often speaking of the negative influences of society that was corruptive and disturbing to him and his family. According to author Vic Dicara, this is the norm for those who are not necessarily Rastafarian and would like to obtain their own levels of spirituality: "Today, Dreadlocks signify spiritual intent, natural and supernatural powers, and are a statement of non-violent non-conformity, communalism and socialistic values, and solidarity with less fortunate or oppressed minorities."

Could anyone understand how such a power was used advantageously in the name of truth and God? According to neighbors and friends, Marcus sincerely felt that he was on the spiritual path of truth and judgment for his family. Alex circa quoted Marcus in a conversation about Christ and the Bible and Christ many years ago, "You know, I just want to live a good life because I want my family to go to heaven, I want to teach my kids the right way, so that we can all go to heaven—I want my family to go to heaven with me. That's why I'm into church, that's why I teach my kids the Bible, that's why I just want them to be healthy, I don't want them really hanging around other kids that can lead my kids the wrong way. The Lord is coming eventually one of these years, sooner than people believe. I just want to be prepared for the coming of Christ."

Steve Morris, the former neighbor and friend to Marcus, also described him in the 1990s' as always respectful to others; teaching his children to be the same way, no matter who they were. Morris said that he and Marcus would have long conversations about God, the Bible and the end of the world. The only glitch that Steve often spoke of was getting Marcus to focus on the "now," living for that very moment in the present, instead of preparing for a future of doom.

Although the follicles and loose strands do not speak words, hair still seems to have its own language of expression, its own power over the individual it dwells. I, for one, cannot assume that it is merely dead waste, growing like a weed...at least religious based facilities don't believe so; author Inejnema Naba wrote:

What is it about hair that is so important for priests and temples? 'It is a notion of purity. Hairs are huge emitters and receptors. When one is in an area, such as a temple, where the flow of energy must be tightly controlled, hair becomes either very helpful or very disturbing, depending on the energetic needs,' Dogon Priest and Kemetic Spiritual Master Naba Lamoussa Morodenibig explained. 'Even when a hair falls off of the body, it does not lose its qualities, and it can become a big disturbance to the flow of energy.'

If one sums up the power of hair, without religion or with it, it is still believed to hold a significant power over a person, even to the point where one looks in the mirror and judges one's own appearance based on the hair. It is no wonder that Marcus Wesson will not cut his hair, for fear that all spiritual power could be lost, making him subjected to Godly punishments, a power he is most fearful of more than anything else. Author Inejnema Naba expanded on this thought when he said:

Perhaps the consequences of breaking even just a few commandments will not be seen in this life, but the sins will be severely punished in the afterlife. One who wears dreadlocks must understand their vow and live up to it, for their own protection...They (commandments) include not getting angry, not gossiping, and not hurting another being, human or non-human. How many of those in the modern societies who have locked hair do not eat meat? How many people with locks do not talk about people behind their backs, gossip, and have hot tempers? How many dreads out there can honestly say that they follow the seventy-seven commandments? Very few!

'People of any race or gender can wear them, because spiritually we are the same,' said Master Naba, 'but the one who has dreadlocks must understand the spiritual meaning behind them if they do not want to face negative consequences.'

Will this be the fate that Marcus now must face, the negative consequences of his past actions as a dreadlock wearer? Most likely, this could be the case. Psychologically, looking past his locks, will bring the public more understanding of how he incorporated such beliefs of power and grandeur into his religious practices and teachings. Although his hair might have brought him the power and confidence to control and master manipulation over family members, it would still be his sanity that would be questionable, as we find in the next chapter.

Those curious locks so aptly twin'd,
Whose every hair a soul doth bind.
~Thomas Carew

"And be not conformed to this world: but be ye transformed by the renewing of your mind, that ye may prove what is that good, and acceptable, and perfect will of God."
~Romans 12:2; *The Bible*

Revelation 9

Psychological Breakdown to Murder

The only fear we are born with is the fear of falling—psychology 101, The Visual Cliff Theory. It is a fact that the only things humans are indistinctively afraid of is heights; we are born with a fear of falling; everything else is learned.

It would be a mistake not to introduce the psychological misfits of Marcus Wesson and the family; that is where all things come together in a neat package, a big bow and pretty wrapping. Irrational reasonings can be explained in detail.

Carmella Johnson, who has a master's degree in psychology and has worked in the field of treating the mentally ill and abuse survivors for about 11 years, is also a therapist with a background as an onsite local elementary school counselor, training rape crisis counselors, and as a family counselor treating families, children, and couples with all sorts of problems. Johnson is well known for her expertise in in-depth counseling, looking beyond the book knowledge to find clearer insight.

Her current emphasis includes providing therapy to adolescents and sex offenders, specializing in treating abuse victims. According to Johnson, some of these abuse victims have become victimizers as they frequently do when the trauma goes untreated.

"In retrospect I would have to say that the most severe cases I have dealt with have been teenagers who, as a result of the severe abuse they suffered, now demonstrate psychotic features," explained Johnson. "The behaviors and cognitive functioning of some of these adolescents adhere to symptomology befitting that of personality, mood, and disassociative disorders. Some people feel that incest and child sexual abuse are not common. Unfortunately it is more common than one would think: One out of four females will be victims of incest or sexual abuse by age 18. One out of every 10 males will be victims of incest or sexual abuse by age 18."

Although there are more cases out there, as stated above, it would be the Wesson case that would draw the most attention—the limelight—because it led to the worst case scenario; murder. The previous statement Johnson made about sexual abuse would explain Marcus Wesson; could he have been sexually violated in his youth, to where he was demonstrating the results of such effects years later? In looking at the power of coping, it is possible that he was able to hold bad memories like these, hoping that the bad dream would finally disappear. Johnson is able to explain the entire development of a child and their influences from their beginning stages; this would explain Marcus who had to have been sexually assaulted at one point in his life and the effects it would have on his children. In the next several pages, she details the cognitive development and impressions that have affected the sexually molested and abused Wesson children; she then goes into the sanity of Marcus Wesson.

The First Influence

Children are influenced by their parents from conception. This influence is not only genetic but environmental as well. Consider this example; a mother who is under a great deal of stress or frequently experiences high levels of anxiety transfers those anxious feelings to her fetus who feels this anxiety as well. When a woman experiences severe emotional stress during her pregnancy, her unborn child is at risk for a wide variety of difficulties. These difficulties range from low miscarriages, premature birth, low birth weight, newborn respiratory illnesses, and difficult temperament. Elevated anxiety levels during the prenatal period have also been associated with physical defects such as Pyloric Stenosis, and Cleft Palate.

Children are shaped both by genetics and nurturing. The shaping of nurturing during the post labor period and on does not always have to come from the biological parent. The individual who provides the primary care and nurturing for the child is known as the primary care giver. The primary care giver then becomes the most influential during the early stages of development. It has been said that a child's personality is formed by the age of seven. The primary caregiver then becomes what could be compared to as the potter and the child the clay. Metaphorically speaking, the potter then begins to mold the child concerning personality, moralities, educational exposure, and so on.

The stages of influence for a child have been debated for decades. The most popular and widely accepted theories of today are that of Jean Piaget's Cognitive Developmental theory and Erick Erickson's theory of Infant and Toddler Emotional Development.

Erickson focused on Psychosocial (personality) development. He hypothesized that a child proceeds through a series of developmental stages in which he must satisfy the desirers that are associated with that particular social need. These stages, desires and needs are explained in the chart on the following page:

See Chart on page 148

As you can see from the chart, a parent/caretaker influences a child in every stage of development. Learning also takes place in every stage and is continuous through out a person's life span.

Take for example the Leaning Tower of Pisa and the cause of its distinctive characteristic. What makes this building so popular is that it is leaning. Even more distinctive is that the lean increases over the decades. The reason the structure is leaning can be traced to errors in its foundation. The building is sinking on one side, which over the centuries increases the lean. Let's use this same line of thinking when considering the importance of the foundation of a child. If a child is raised in a home where he/she learns it is not safe to trust others, their foundation becomes one of distrusting others. If a child is emotionally abused during the first 12 years of the life, their foundation is then constructed of the elements of the

Erick Erickson's theory of Infant and Toddler Emotional Development.

Stage Name	Trust vs Mistrust	Autonomy vs Shame & doubt	Initiative vs Guilt	Industry vs Inferiority	Identity vs Role confusion	Intimacy vs Isolation
Age Range	Birth to age 1	1 to 3 years	3 to 5 years	5 to 12 years	Adolescence	20 to 40 years
Desires	To trust in caregiver and world	Forming since of independence	Becoming ambitious showing usefulness	Sense of accomplishment	Establishing personal identity	Commit to an intimate partner
Negative Outcome	Distrustful of others	Feelings of shame towards self	Criticism = timid and fearful view	Feeling inferior to peers	Not knowing who you are	Wanted & needed by a partner

abuse. The leaning Tower of Pisa leans further and further towards its destruction every year due to its unstable foundation. Just as the Tower will eventually fall, so will a child who's foundation is irreparable. There is no repairing the tower because its foundation is too deeply rooted and the tower is much too large. Once a foundation is set, it by common understanding is permanent. In order for it to be repaired it would have to be broken down totally, and rebuilt. The questions then become: is this possible with humans, and what are the means by which this could be accomplished?

The Age of Impressions

Children are impressionable at every age. Through my research, work with clients and personal observations I truly believe that damage done to a child during the first 10 years of life prove to be the most difficult from which to heal. The first four to five years are the foundations of a child's personality and view of the world. These foundational years are those of shaping and forming a child. Forming refers to the way a child feels about himself and others, the view a child develops of his world, and where he fits in that world. The environment that a child has the most contact with is typically the family unit. When this statement is true, the family then becomes the environment that has the most influential impact on the child. When a child is not with his family then the group of people with whom the child resides and receives care giving and the basic necessities of life, then become the family of influence. In every family environment there is a culture that contains a set of rules, language, norms and unacceptable actions. As an infant, an individual observes this culture and the way others move and interact within this set of rules, his schema is formed. They observe that the more effective a person fits into these norms, the more favorable the consequences for that particular individual. Therefore, less that a person fits in with these norms or the more they break the rules of engagement, the more negative the consequences, again for that particular individual. As this child passes through the stages of cognitive development, he acquires his own way of navigating through the norms and unacceptable actions. He is careful to observe and adhere to the rules, and norms as not to experience any of the negative consequences he has observed. A metaphorical way of viewing this would be to liken the situation to a child learning a language. He learns the grammar, syntax, and bad words of that language. Once the child begins to interact with those outside of the home, he tends to speak the language that he is accustomed to speaking. He does not understand why others do not understand what he is saying, or that they do not speak the same language. Even once this child grows up and learns the "other" language," when a stressful situation arises for the child, he or she becomes comfortable, he/she tends to begin to speak his native language. There are even situations where the child learns the other language but continues to incorporate the syntax and grammar rules of his childhood language. This results in the individual exhibiting behaviors that are not understood by others in society.

Past the Point of No Return

In looking at the Wesson daughters and nieces who have survived, one wonders if they will ever find normalcy in society's views of wrong and rights in dating, love and unconditional love for parents. Perhaps they are too far past the point of no return...

We then have an enigma when we consider the question, "Is there a point of no return?" The question can then be asked, "Return from what?" The child does not realize that there is actually a place to return to because she has never been there. We are then faced with the exercise of adding additional programming that has the capability of over writing the old information without deleting the positive lessons that can be incorporated into the new scheme of thinking and feeling.

As a person grows up and interacts with those outside of the home, she assumes that the same cultural rules apply, so she behaves as if she is still in that same culture. When and if the person's behavior will cause problems in the individual becomes the next question. Very often we see the behavior causing distress in the child's school-age years. This is the time when they began to form relationships outside of the home and interact with people of authority. The cultural rules of the school do not coincide with those in the home;

therefore, the child finds it difficult to navigate through the cultural norms without hitting bumps and causing himself to be noticed in an unfavorable manner. This then causes more anxiety in the child. It also causes her peers and those in authority to have negative feelings. When these people act on their negative feelings, the child becomes even more distressed. Once again, she will revert even further into behaviors that are familiar, creating another round in the cycle of distress and display of what is now termed "dysfunctional behaviors." These behaviors are only dysfunctional because they are being displayed in a foreign culture. Imagine a child that spoke a foreign language that you were not familiar with. If that child attempted to ask you if you had any chocolate milk in his native tongue, most likely he would never have his request granted. Why? The answer is very simple; you do not know what the child is trying to say. Now he is getting frustrated, and so are you because he wants chocolate milk, but you won't give it to him because you don't have the slightest idea of what he is saying. This is often what happens when children from abusive homes interact with others outside of their culture of abuse. Is there hope for these children? Of course! We are all a work in progress.

Coping Strategies for Repeated Molestation

When confronted with situations that overload our coping abilities, we as humans tend to form coping strategies. These coping strategies help us to lighten the blow or to absorb a little less of the pain that these situations cause. Coping strategies are often learned by observation. If a child sees that his parents or care-givers drink to dull the pain, then he or she learns that drinking dulls the pain. Despite seeing that the drinking also causes pain, he learns that drinking is a viable method of coping. Below are a list of coping strategies that are frequently used by children and adults alike when dealing with childhood abuse.

See Chart on next page...

Coping Strategies

Acting out	Cutting	Drugs	Sexual acting out	Keeping busy
Drinking alcohol	Starving ones self/Over eating	Excessive sleeping	Verbal/Physical aggression	Relentless joking and sarcasm
Insomnia	Withdrawal	Blocking out	Distracting	Denial
Disassociating	Rationalizing	Emotional Cut off	Psychosomatic Illness	Having a since of entitlement and control

These coping strategies manifest themselves in a variety of situations. At times those outside of the abusive situation may view these coping strategies as insanity or sickness. It is easy to judge from the outside when we are not directly experiencing the situation ourselves. For some of these children the reality of this abuse being wrong does not exist. It is the only reality they know. This lack of knowledge then becomes ignorance as opposed to the coping strategy of denial. There are tribes in Africa who drink blood as a normal part of a healthy diet. For the normal U.S. population, drinking blood would be considered immoral. To the people of these tribes it is considered normal. For others to go into their culture and tell them that this action is wrong would not be understood. They would have trouble understanding how something they have grown up with all their lives could be wrong. This same explanation can be applied to children from abusive homes. Because this abusive behavior is normal for these children, the absence of abuse is abnormal for them. Research has shown that often children from abusive homes, when taken out of these homes, will behave in ways that provoke others to display the abusive behaviors to which they are accustomed.

Understanding How Children Interpret Abuse

As children pass through the various stages of development they gain additional information and they assimilate the new information into their existing areas of information and reasoning. To gain a better understanding of how abuse affects a child we will use the picture in figure 1. This picture could be considered the brain of an average 9 year-old child. According to Erickson, this child would be in the industry vs inferiority stage of cognitive development. As one can see, the child has already gained the information required to pass through the previous developmental stages.

Now let's picture the words encircling the child as being in different situations the child encounters. The arrows show how these situations are accommodated and assimilated into the various cognitive areas of understanding. Pay attention to where the abuse situations might be absorbed. Notice that there are no compartments for deciphering abuse. Because a child has no cognitive area of understanding abusive situations, these actions are dispersed into other compartments such as love, acceptance, and inferiority.

Let's say for example a child interprets sexual touching as a form of showing love. This child then may grow up feeling that a normal way of showing love to others would be to fondle their gentiles. The child is not in control of how he or she interprets the acts. It is the person committing the acts who often times tells the child how to assimilate the actions into their cognitive understanding. This individual may not verbally tell the child how to interpret the information; however, the status they hold with the child represents how the information should be interpreted. For example, love comes from a mother, father, and other family members, so the actions these family members exhibit may be understood as actions of love. Another example of a child's interpretation of situations is that of visiting a friend's house. If the child is accepted and treated pleasantly during the visit, there is a good chance that he/she will interpret this information as meaning acceptance. When their physical and psychological needs are met, a child interprets these as meaning trust and stability. Just as a child assimilates and accommodates positive stimuli into pre-existing cognitive understanding, negative stimuli are processed in the same manner.

See diagram next page

Do the Wesson children know when sexual abuse is wrong, despite if a parent is telling them otherwise?

The age of the onset of the molestation is a great factor in whether the child realizes that the act of sex is wrong between adults and children. The earlier the act takes place, *the harder it will be for the child to determine that the act is wrong*. In addition, the more frequent the act occurs, the more difficulty the child has when determining the wrongness in the act of molestation. Now add in the factor of who the molester is. If the perpetrator is a parent, care giver or someone who the child feels loves or cares for him, like Marcus, a father, the boundaries of right and wrong now become so blurred

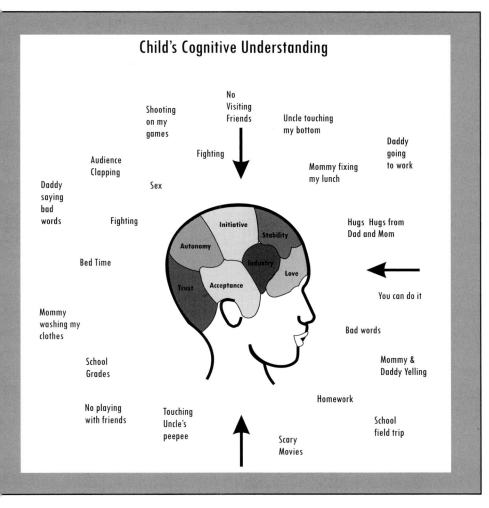

Child's Cognitive Understanding

that they are often virtually nonexistent. Unfortunately, this blurred vision is compounded when added to the equation that the molester is telling the child this is an act of love or that this act is perfectly normal between father and daughter or adult and child.

Imagine that you grew up all your life eating meat. As you were growing up, your parents taught you that eating meat was good for you, some times you didn't really like it, but to be a good little boy or girl you ate all your meat. Now, imagine that when you become an adult someone came along and told you, it is wrong for you to eat meat. In fact they not only told you it was wrong to eat meat, they also told you that meat was not good for you and that your mommy and daddy don't really love you because they fed you meat. Imagine if they literally told you that being fed meat was abusive. Do you think this idea would be easy for you to adopt?

There is another disturbing factor that further complicates the act of sexual abuse. If the child is in a sexual relationship with an adult in which she is being seduced, the act then becomes more difficult to heal from. Often, child sexual abusers will seduce the child, which on the surface makes the child a willing participant. Notice the words, "on the surface." The child is not a willing participant because he/she does not possess the cognitive abilities required to decipher the behaviors of the abuser as wrong. Picture the abuser simply starting the abuse with loving touches here and there. Later these loving touches are on the breast or buttocks. As time goes on the kisses then go from a gentle peck on the cheek to the mouth. Within a few years the kissing becomes full blown oral penetration. Slowly but surely the touching has changed from mere touching to fondling of the vagina, with a focus on the clitoris. Despite being uncomfortable psychologically, the child is being stimulated physically—this act occurred among the Wesson daughters and nieces. Once this type of fondling happens, the child has a very difficult time realizing this type of touching is wrong because she is being told this is an act of love, in addition to physical pleasure involved. If a lack of outside exposure exists telling child that this behavior is wrong, he/she may never come to realize the immoral nature of the act, despite some where inside feeling a level of remorse and sever distress.

The Silence of the Wesson Nieces and Daughters

It is very hard for the public to understand why the Wesson children didn't say anything to anyone as they were growing up in the household. Of course a few of the girls ran away in their teens, but that does not give us an understanding of why they didn't do something earlier. Carmella Johnson explores these issues with a list of questions and explanations as if the girls were the ones responding; coming from a psychological basis.

From the mind of a child...

Why didn't the children tell someone they were being abused?

This answer lies within the mind of understanding; one must place himself in the world of this child: Who exactly do you tell? A frightened child will not tell his uncle or aunt, "Marcus is having sex with me." What is sex? Does a child know what sex is at ages 7, 8, and 9?

Who do I tell, when for years I have been taught the police, and anyone like them are of Satan. If I tell, will they come get me and take me away? Take me where? Take me away from my family, no please don't, then I will be all alone. If they do come to take us, we all have to kill ourselves, don't we have to kill ourselves?

Other questions probably on these children's minds were; *Who do I tell? I can't talk to men. If I do, I'll be punished! It hurts too bad to be hit again and again, over and over. I can't tell, I have no where to go. It's not that bad. Uncle Marcus loves me and shows me special attention. As long as I am good, and I do what I am told, everything will be okay.*

For some, the question of, "why not just tell?" may seem like a mystery. In the minds of frightened confused children, telling is the absolutely worst thing they could do. How hard it must be to be pulled out of school and taken away from friends, having no idea why. Imagine having a mother who is a drug addict, and as a child you and your sisters have to take care of each other. That is, until Uncle Marcus and Aunt Elizabeth allow you to live with them.

Why tell now? Why did it take so long for the Solorio nieces to come forward with these hidden issues?

I have to tell now! I have to get it out! All this time I wasn't allowed to talk to anyone outside my home. If we did, my cousins and sisters, were sure to be beaten, over and over again. Consequences like being stabbed in the chest, were real. Remember what happened to Sophia when she ran away. Consequences like being blamed for tearing the family apart, I can't do that, I have to go to heaven.

Can a person cope with that kind of hardship? Is it really an easy task to tell a complete stranger that you have sex with your sisters, but you don't want to? To tell opens one up to the shame, the judgment of those who do not like one's way of living, those who don't follow Christ. The nieces might have felt then: *Marcus is Christ, and he saved us. He saved us from our mom who didn't take care of us. He saved us from the schools who only wanted to teach us bad things. He told us what to do if "Satan," the police ever came for us. We can't tell on Marcus, he is our savior.*

Can, I tell now? Will you listen? I have to tell, I have to get it out. If I tell you, will you help me? Will you blame me for all that has happened? My children are gone, but they weren't really my children, I had them for God. Wasn't I supposed to do that? No, I didn't want to, but that was because I was being selfish. Wasn't I?

The answers are not simple, when you place yourself in the world of an abused child, a world where "what I thought was right is not right," because the reality of it all is, they never really knew what was right.

Why didn't I tell? I don't know, I know what kept me alive. I do know who fed me. I know who allowed me to stay in my home. I know who took me in when my mother wasn't taking care of me and my sisters. I know who loves me enough to give himself to me. Marcus loves me, he told me he loves me. I must be good, it hurts too bad not to. Can, I talk now? Please let me talk now!

The Process of Healing

What is the worst case scenario of a child that has been heavily influenced and molested by a parent for years? Can they change?

Unfortunately, the worst case I feel would be becoming a serial rapist or a child molester. Whether or not a person changes relies on the individual. If a person does not have a heart to change, no amount of therapy can work. Not even castration is guaranteed to extinguish the desire to engage in some type of sexual activity. On the other hand, if the individual grows to realize that engaging in any type of sexual activity with a child is wrong, and is able to connect with deeper levels of remorse for his/her actions, then change becomes a possibility. The type of treatment and therapy then becomes another factor in the desired level and duration of change.

The journey to healing is a life-long endeavor that begins with the recognition that something is inherently wrong. As this child interacts with others and speaks his language of behavior, he observes that the behaviors he used to navigate through life at home are not acceptable in the outside world. An even deeper problem arises when the rules of the outside world do not permit the language but the same grammatical rules and syntax of his native language are seen on television, heard in music and rewarded in certain public arenas. This subject matter is too broad and must be tackled in another setting.

Prison of Restrictions in Adulthood Resulting from Childhood Abuse

When an individual suffers from childhood abuse they continue to be in bondage to the abuse until they realize that they are indeed in bondage and begin taking the steps to release themselves from such bondage. The restrictions of this bondage are more often not physical bondages, but bondages of the mind and soul. For example consider the training of an elephant. When an elephant is born in captivity and will be trained to perform, he is chained up as a baby. The elephant is chained to a spike that is nailed to the ground. The elephant then grows up in this bondage, knowing that no matter how hard he tries, he can never go further than what the chain or the trainer will allow. As the elephant grows in the physical strength needed to break free, he diminishes in will power to become free. Once the will to be free is totally broken, the chains can come off. Now, despite being free, the elephant has the perception that he can go no further than what the chain or the trainer allows, thus the elephant remains in captivity in what appears to be his own will. Let us take this one step further. If by some chance the elephant does become free, he will yearn to return to his bondage because it is not perceived as bondage, but as home. While out of captivity the elephant will try just as humans do, to apply the rules of a culture of captivity, to a culture of "normalcy." Once again, just as humans, he will act out and hurt others around him in an effort to return to a since of familiarity, a place of bondage, a place called home.

The Psychology of Marcus Wesson

In appearance, Marcus Wesson comes across as a sane man, intelligent and yet able to speak his words intelligently with etiquette and politeness, proving that as a black male he has just as much smarts as anyone else. Underneath this façade is another world, created by him as a coping mechanism to deal with the cruel world that had tailored his thoughts and actions in wanting to be an able, productive citizen. Instead, he is a recluse, cornered by societal restrictions, hurt by the anxieties of life; disturbed by the world's presence.

In relation to the prosecution who is gearing up for this case by getting a number of psychologist involved, this may not be the wisest thing, according to Johnson; it doesn't always prove that someone is sane or insane…

"Although I am in no way doubting the capabilities of the psychologist involved, getting a plethora of professionals involved as the prosecution would suggest is not a solve all. Just because a psychologist is skillful in a particular area, doesn't mean they are just as superior in another. Most therapists have an expertise; an area in which they are innately gifted to address and treat. An aspect in the field of psychology that is both negative and positive is that we are all wearing different eye glasses, with different color lenses and points of view. For example; a person can look at the same picture as 10 other people and see it differently. This is because we each have what I term as 'the glass of life.' Our experiences and exposures form our glasses. The lenses are then colored by the view we form of these experiences, and therefore add the color by which we view our lives. I may see the world from a pink point of view, while others may view it as blue."

In explaining Marcus, Johnson said the following:

The man is not going to be considered incompetent to stand trial because he is able to understand the charges being placed against him. He is also able to assist his lawyers in preparing his defense. However, I do feel that he has a mental disorder that prevents him from knowing right from wrong. In speaking with his family and reading some of his statements, it is clear to me that Marcus Wesson, nor his immediate family members, had a clear understanding that what he did was wrong. It may be fascinating to people that in his world and the world that he created for his family that he is Jesus. If he feels that his behavior is right because he hears God telling him to marry his daughters and nieces and that they were meant to have children by him (Jesus being Marcus), for God, then we have a problem. He doesn't, seem to know that having sexual intercourse with his children is wrong; his children do not see this as wrong either.

Despite being able to speak intelligently and being able to interact with others on an intellectual level, not to mention appearing to be charismatic on some level according to the DSM (Diagnostic Statistical Manual), he *can* fit the basic criteria for schizophrenia. He had delusions of grandeur as displayed by his telling his family that he was Jesus. He also had delusions of persecution in which he felt like the *system* was out to get him and his children. He also had auditory hallucinations in which he said that God told him to father children by his daughters and nieces. There was also a display of negative symptoms in which he displayed a reduced range in emotion and expression. If you pay close attention to Mr. Wesson, at times it appears that something is missing from him. The problem lies in determining the extent of these symptoms. Some may argue that he is not mentally ill or insane because he displays what some would consider a normal to high level of intelligence. This fact is true because his handicap does not lie in that area. His dysfunction is displayed in his marked inability to hold employment, socialize with others outside of his immediate family, and his noticeable deterioration of hygiene. When it comes to the treatment of others, he does not see the difference between right and wrong, he does not see it. Ask him not to control someone he loves, he can't do it, because that's all he knows.

In court, Marcus is looking at this entire situation as the whole outside world is coming against his way of life because he has certain strong ideals and beliefs. He feels justified for what he did. That's the tricky thing about it: at one point, he didn't pull the trigger, but he was in the room when it happened. Although he says he didn't do it, was he responsible? As powerful as he is, in the prosecution's mind, he could have snapped his fingers and his family would have jumped. So to them he still had the control to stop it; he allowed it to happen.

Sanity is very subjective. The legal stand point of law states that a person is legally insane if they cannot tell the difference between right or wrong, or if they have a mental illness preventing them from being able to control themselves and therefore follow the law. On the surface, Marcus is capable of standing trial. But one cannot judge the health of a tree based on the outside. He went far beyond being sexually attracted to children as in the case of a pedophile who gains sexual gratification by observing, or engaging in sexual acts with pubescent children. There was a method to the sexual madness of Marcus Wesson. He did not penetrate his daughters or his nieces with his penis until they were teenagers. Even then he purposefully did not allow them to have his children until they were age 18, and he held a private marriage ceremony legitimizing in his mind the act of having children.

I would see him (Marcus) in stores, walk past him, and ask myself what is in him? Each time I saw him, I intentionally attempted to make eye contact, but he would not look me eye to eye, he would look past me. I wanted to look in his eyes, but he would not allow himself to make contact with me in this manner. As I reflect on one of these occasions, I recall being in a local store, my dress was professional, as well as my whole demeanor and attitude, I complimented him by remarking that his hair locks were extraordinary. He glanced at me and said, "Thank you," and almost instinctively turned away very quickly. I thought to myself, I wonder if his eye contact is determined by the context in which he views you?

I believe there is a large portion of this man that is trapped in his childhood. I also believe if we were able to thoroughly explore his life as a child, we would find out when and how he was abused. In my opinion Marcus Wesson posses attributes of control that are inherent of grooming. Somewhere in his life—via observation or experience—he was taught how to control others. At some point in his life, I think he lacked total control over himself, and to protect his psyche he now dramatically over compensates for that loss. Though we may not have all of the pieces to the puzzle, if we dig, I believe we will find a time in Marcus Wesson's life in which he had some horrific experiences that exceeded his coping capabilities. Something happened to change this man who is described by his mother as being a normal church going child, into the monster who could do the hideous things of which he is being accused.

Simply stated; we all change according to our exposure. What we change into is determined by the seeds that have been planted in our lives. Despite falling through the cracks of authorities, Marcus Wesson possessed the seeds of destruction. The acts that occurred on March 12th are the proverbial leaves of the trees which popped above the soil of his life in plain sight for the world to see. Just as a giant Oak tree who's roots destroy a neatly crafted   side walk and ruin the plumbing of a beautiful home, so do the roots of destruction and devastation; the tree and Mr. Wesson run deep and are strong.

The Wesson Family Members, they are all victims, of themselves and or their pasts. An overwhelming percent of murderers and rapist in prison were exposed to pornography and abuse in childhood. Children do not possess a place for sex in their cognitive understanding; as a result, if not directed by a loving parent, the information is accommodated into areas where it does not belong. Unless we as a society figure out how to control what our children are exposed to and gain a better understand of the effects of exposure to sex, violence and abuse, we will undoubtedly face more of these types of cases. Who's to say that you the reader won't wake up tomorrow to find you have neighbors like the Wessons, the same scenario gone too far—gone to murder…

The Definition of a Mass Murderer

Contrary to psychologist and therapist Carmella Johnson's position on the insanity of Marcus, in a personal interview with Dr. Hickey, it was well noted that Marcus was less of a mental case and more of a cultist; "It's pretty hard to thwart a mass murder, mass murderers tend to be people who are insane or have some kind of mental illness. In this case it wasn't a mental illness; it was a cult issue where I suspect that he had land in his mind, he decided that he would never give up his children. And when the day came that he might have to, he would simply have to kill them himself..."

According to Dr. Hickey, there was no warning of what was to come from the Wesson household; there was no record on file of Marcus being abusive to his children in the CPS or police files. This would make it hard for the police to consider the scene that was to take place of no more than a domestic dispute over parenting and children—not mass murder.

"He wasn't calling the police, saying he killed his kids," explained Dr. Hickey "He didn't give any warning. It was just very private. Long before that day happened, there probably should have been more attention paid when he was living in the Bay Area . He was living out of bathrooms then. He's the kind of guy that to me, from what I read, a very bright man, very capable, and very influential to certain people—primarily women—and was able to manipulate and get what he wanted and knew the system very well."

Wesson was able to slip through the cracks of the system unnoticed, remarked Dr. Hickey. "A lot of people have done far worse than Mr. Wesson when it came to not taking care of their children. So the police, they hear and they compare what he's doing—okay, he's got all these women surrounding him and so on—but what you hear from other cases is far more serious. I don't see how they could have foreseen that murder scene."

What fits the profile of a mass murder? According to Hickey, usually not a black man. Dr. Hickey identified in his book *Serial Murderers and Their Victims*, most offenders are primarily white, male and encompass a wide age range. He also said in the personal interview, "How many black mass murders do you see? Pretty rare. Almost all are white. I've got a handful of blacks, but there's very few blacks that are mass murderers, especially with domestic violence. You find more whites being sex offenders; you find more blacks doing robberies. Philadelphia, he killed a whole bunch of people, police officers—Gregory Lett."

However mass murderers certainly have a history of violence, something Marcus did not have. "He's an oddity from the way I look at him because he wasn't one to fit that mass murder profile," said Dr. Hickey. " ... They usually have a lot of anger, I don't know if he had a lot of anger, maybe he did. But what he did have was this David Koresh kind of thinking, he had this Jim Jones kind of thinking. He in his own world was his supreme ruler. Outside the world he learned to adapt how to get around the system. But in his own kingdom, the females walked 10 paces behind him. He ruled and maybe he ruled with kindness, but nobody was going to take his kids away from him. What complicated it was because he had so many different women... So it gave him sense of supremacy. You don't see that a lot in mass murderers."

Split between a domestic dispute within the family or internal issues displayed in the public, usually the mind of a mass murderer will feel that he or she has to solve these issues by inflicting harm on others.

"There's only been a handful of mass murderers who kill like that who murder people in their family in the United States; maybe 2, no more than 3, 4, 5 cases."

In his book, Dr. Hickey stated, "an ideological mass murderer is a person, especially a cult leader, who is able to persuade others to kill themselves or each other, as in the cases of Jim Jones (Jonestown Massacre), Herff Applewhite (Heaven's Gate), and David Koresh (Waco Massacre)." This definition defines Marcus's accusations in regards to the murders, the coercion of the acts, not the acts of murder.

Some of the identifiable characteristics of a mass murderer are not conclusive, according to Dr. Hickey: "...Isolation, anger, paranoia— again this will vary but these you often will see—they can be hyper-vigilant, very controlling, spontaneous. They tend to be isolated in society, they tend to be in a loner state; they don't feel any loss or loneliness, their framework of the world is different on how they see the world." Perhaps some of these characteristics would fit Mr. Wesson in his controlling state of the women he manipulated in the household. Although Elizabeth denies such forms of control by her husband Marcus, Dr. Hickey noted that most of the time they do not realize they are being controlled.

"The women are compliant, the women have been manipulated, used and controlled and that's very common in cults. Marcus Wesson didn't control a lot of men, did he? It's always the women they control; unfortunately... women looking for a leader, looking for a power figure, they're looking for a man because they want to be controlled. There are some women like that. To this day, they (Wesson daughters, wives and nieces) still support him, he's still their leader—that's common. A lot of psychological mind control takes place with these people, so they truly believe that their leader is a good guy, that he's not a bad person. And even if he did do the killings, it was for a higher power, for better reasoning that we don't understand. They don't have the same mind frame."

Dr. Hickey suggested that the main wife, Elizabeth, may have known what was going on but had no control over that situation; as psychologist Johnson stated before, she may not have known there was anything wrong with their lifestyle.

"Cults work differently in a Jim Jones society. She(Elizabeth) may have known, she may have had a sense of what he would do if it was necessary, but he was in charge. Maybe they were in denial about it, and felt like he wouldn't do that, he just does that to make lovers and keep control of them. I don't think that she told him to do it at all; that's what she had to live with—the incest was rampant. There's a group in Utah,--1,500 of them—very similar to this situation."

The details slowly add up: Marcus; a cultist leader, controlling yet docile, insane in his pattern and approach to premeditated genocide by divine right, yet sane in his actions of getting prior consent to have sex with his daughters and nieces, making them his wives. Could this be a new profile of a murderer with sane traits, but insane motives? In the loneliness of his mind, society was not right for him or his family; this notion was taken to an extreme to create his world for the safety of his family—allowing the insanity to appear very sane.

As we explore Elizabeth's side of the story in the next revelation, a woman with much grief, she never appears to be the victim of manipulation in her words; yet in a funny way, it can still be noticed the damage her husband thwarted to her. The mystery of the unknown as to the why this happened would be a puzzling fact and memory she would have to deal with for an eternity.

> *In a disturbed mind, as in a body in the same state,*
> *health can not exist.*
> ## ~Cicero (Marcus Tullius Cicero)

"In Rama was there a voice heard, lamentation, and weeping, and great mourning, Rachel weeping for her children, and would not be comforted, because they are not."
~Matthew, 2:18; *The Bible*

Revelation 10

A Mother's Song; The Elizabeth Tone

It was a hot late July; almost four and half months after the March 12th Wesson homicides. Wasn't it time we had a better understanding of Marcus Wesson and his family? Our research had entailed all of the basic detail and anatomy of the murder; yet questions remain about the family dynamics behind it. Had we not been curious about them, a very different book would have been written; a very different story would have been told.

It was July 28, 2004 when we headed down to the Fresno County Court House in hopes of finding more information about the family. We had attempted to contact them before; sending a letter of our intent but there was no response. We had seen them on TV enough to sense that they were a close-knit, reserved family distraught by circumstances. This was confirmed over time. There had already been enough media and people to invade their private world with curiosity and mediocre news stories of disappointment. We had one unifying idea, that maybe we could see behind the screen of the TV and into the truth, for ourselves; seeing them in person would have a formidable effect.

We walk into the courtroom, and sit down intently observing the energy in the room. It just so happens we sit down behind Kiani Wesson and Rosie Solorio, the daughter and niece of Marcus Wesson who mothered two children each for him. Their bodies are quite stationary, and fixed on the man in question sitting in the front of the courtroom with his public defender Pete Jones. They are in the third pew, intermittently shedding quiet tears as they glance at him now and then. The media daintily approaches them, leaning over toward them in whispers, asking if they would like to make a statement. With an innocent and calming smile, Kiani politely tells the media, that there is no statement as this time. Kiani was often seen as the outspoken one on the news making statements to defend her family and accused father. However this time, her mood is humble, looking for a certain peace in a chaotic space. Rosie smiles supportively with Kiani in response to the media's inquiry.

The atmosphere is strained; three court sheriffs stand eyeing each corner of the room. One stands with his arms folded, swaying sometimes back and forth then leaning one arm on the county clerk's courtroom desk. Marcus Wesson is wearing all black, it is clear that he has lost a few pounds since his last television image. A bike-style linked metal chain centers around his waist, enveloping his belly and lower back, then encircling around each arm. He tries to write notes on the case as his attorney and prosecution fight with knockout blows relating to the questions on the jury questionnaire to be distributed in several months. The chains seem effervescent, as each stroke of the pen flows without difficulty; rhythmic chain sounds gently tap the desk as he writes, fitting into the melody of the courtroom.

In the argument, Pete Jones vigorously defends that African-Americans have a history of being racially discriminated against by our penal system, and he is willing to prove it. The prosecution denies the claim, identifying Mr. Jones as going over board on this issue. As they continue back and forth, my husband Lennice takes notice of Serafino, the younger son of Marcus Wesson. He sits impatiently to the left of us, attempting to get his sister, Kiani's attention to tell her he has to go and wants her to leave too. She insists on staying. Lennice clues in on the situation and decides to have a few words with Serafino, also known as "Fino." During a court recess, Lennice steps outside with Fino and then comes back inside to tell me that he's going to drop Fino off at school. This is no surprise to me because I know Lennice has a gift of striking up conversations with strangers who find comfort in telling him their life stories. This explained Fino's impatience, worried about class because he had missed so many at a local adult school facility where he was hoping to receive his high school diploma in the weeks ahead.

As they left, I followed the interaction of Kiana and the court appointed assistant to the family. Overhearing the conversation, I was privileged to hear about their many talents; Kiani who loves to write and Rosie who said they both had a lot of restaurant experience. I was trying to decipher the sincerity of the conversation; were the courts exploiting these naïve young ladies to get more information or was it a genuine attempt to help them move on with their lives and find jobs? I began to worry about this fact and found a need to step in after the court family liaison was finished. I had previously written them a note about interviewing them in regard to this case. I had slipped the note to them, letting them know who Lennice and I were. At first, thinking that we were the television or newspaper media, they politely responded that they would not be giving any statements at this time. I assured them that our inquiry was different. While in casual conversation, they began to realize who I was and recall the letter we had sent. Although tentative, they were willing to know more about our intentions. I proceeded to ask them about their backgrounds—but it was at that moment my perspective changed. I found myself becoming increasingly aware of their needs and their situation. My attitude of just getting the facts seemed incomplete, more was needed. Underneath the enduring public smiles were impending needs. Money was scarce and apparently an issue right now. Their bread winner was on trial. Their main mother Elizabeth and remaining siblings were terribly distraught over the loved ones who were dead. I suggested they call me in hopes to connect them with people who could help them find work. They were willing to do any service job; cooking, any restaurant job—whatever could bring in an income, but out of the limelight. They even had interests in going to school; their younger sister Gypsy was enjoying such a privilege in taking night courses to finish her diploma.

What was I thinking! The teacher in me couldn't help but give a helping hand, the teacher in me couldn't help but find a way to give these young ladies a way to survive—then I could continue on with our book, I thought. No one can give a clear thought or interview in such a situation without an income, I assumed. They were like children I couldn't neglect; I would have done the same for the students at my school—and have done so. The humanitarian side of me took over, and that is where our relationship with the Wesson family began.

Shortly after, Lennice came back and it was apparent that the humanitarian, teacher-side took him over as well; the next thing I knew, he was setting up appointments to tutor Fino in math. Our quest had changed from the average researcher to civil citizens doing a service for other citizens in need. We didn't want this to affect our research but we didn't want to see a family be starved out due to ignorance and a lack of assistance. My mind toiled with this fact, knowing that somewhere we would have to draw the line; our minds were focused on a project involving their family and murder. We finally felt the best way to handle the situation was to be honest; let the family know of our intentions but also help them get on their feet.

Although Lennice was more so into the many conversations with Fino, developing a friendship, we all pitched in to help with the basic needs. Colleagues and friends helped us obtain food from nonprofit organizations and temporary clothing; as the family was still wearing the same clothes on their backs from the night of the murder and some donated clothing due to the seizure of evidence by the police department, protocol for mass murder cases like this. It turns out that all of their clothes were in the house or on the motor home bus. Without judgment, we helped as best we could with any family in need, no matter the circumstances. Lennice worked and worked with Fino who was behind in his basic math skills, but was attempting to pass his exam for his GED anyway. He also tried to find Fino a job, just so that he could have a bite to eat—there was no luck. There was too much judgment in this town and Fino was getting desperate to help himself and his family. Some jobs we were able to provide were ready to hire Fino; however, he did not have identification: a social security card or a driver's license. That made things very difficult. A lot of his things were also confiscated from the house or the bus. Finally Lennice helped him get the identification needed. As innocence was his barrier, he was upfront with employers about not having job experience, just having under the table jobs to get by; this of course hurt him as well and became a major disappointment to him and ourselves. We soon found more road blocks because of his educational level; and still others would create excuses once they saw his last name filled out on the application. The story was never ending and tiresome to the point where Lennice, himself, felt very discouraged, helpless, and demoralized using all of the connections that just weren't coming through for him.

The times were becoming more desperate and money was still scarce. Lennice began to grow an attachment to Fino, wanting him to be able to have a job and pass the GED test, which Lennice was not hopeful because of his basic math level—he was too far behind the general math curve. He was aware of Fino's conditions: worrying about food, a place to stay, what's going on with his father, what to do next, what will happen to him. The anguishes were piling on this young man of 19 who was naively entering the cruel, unforgiving world. The world often talked about by his father who tried to shield him from these things and by doing so ultimately only hindered him, crippling his insides, his hopes, morale and self-esteem. Facing such harshness created anger in Fino who would find ways to release these emotions in karate class. Other times he would keep his feelings all balled up, turn red or go on long walks to sort his distorted thoughts and compacted realities. Fino had the friendly, respectful personality that prompted anyone to want to help him; no matter the circumstance. He would be very appreciative of Lennice's assistance and ours and never stopped thanking us. There would be days Fino would go without eating, and yet one would never know: keeping it private because it would be rude to beg for food or to ask, even if one was starving or so he was raised. His undertones of hunger never came through in his speech; for his expressions were passionate and curious. In his eyes there was deep pain rooted underneath his glassy stare that simply wanted to know why, that simply wanted to escape these grown-up pressures. Ironically he was not realizing that everyone else in society viewed him as an adult. He was still a learning child, coping with an overwhelming situation. Who else has to deal with these kinds of extremes; being painted an outcast, judged because of the apparent actions of a family member, and part of an abandoned family buckling under the weight of social shunning?

Fino would often state that he just wanted a normal life; wanted to go into the military, unafraid of battle. Not having his GED or high school diploma and confronted with a brewing, high-profile case tarnished all of these dreams into successful nightmares. These are the simple things people take for granted; an education, a low-end job or food. Not this young man; a car ride listening to the radio was joyous and a treat, going to the movies to watch a karate flick or having a sit-down meal at Denny's were delights treasured and remembered.

It was soon after spending time with the outgoing and gregarious Fino that the timid Elizabeth decided to meet with us. Not concerned about her own situation which was grim, Elizabeth was thankful that we were trying to help her son Fino, and she simply wanted to meet us to thank us, especially Lennice, for what we were trying to do. She felt that he was the one son that needed the most guidance and was the most trusting of everyone; which was a problem when they encountered the media. Apparently Elizabeth and her family felt mislead by the objective of a local Fresno television station news reporter who promised them one thing and delivered another. The reporter was more targeted on the shocking incest related details of the case, while the Wesson family was led to believe they would be interviewed about who they were; their family background. Upset and bewildered, Elizabeth took a huge step backwards, secluding herself from all media, associations and fake friends yearning to get close for a small peep. It's almost as if the Wesson family was the community science project; specimens of a greater experiment to be dissected and made an example. They were being prodded and pressured from all angles by people who wanted to get a good story by their editor's deadlines. She was explaining her fears and what had happened to her when she did try to talk about her family who were very different; it certainly didn't come out the way she expected. They were ridiculed on the local news. She decided to block everyone out and go within to find peace. This was her best strategy for a mother in mourning who also had to grieve for her husband's detainment, trial, and possible death sentence.

It was her son Fino who had told her about us and how helpful we were to him and the family. She was tired of bending for people she thought she could trust; every time to get snubbed. This time, she took a chance.

Elizabeth and I started out conversing on the phone. She was very careful about what she was saying to me and equally cautious about where we would meet, paranoid about the media, detectives and other predators. With honesty and directness, I let her know that it was myself and business partners who wrote her the letter several months prior to actually meeting with her and her family. What I didn't realize is what that letter probably meant to her at the time; what it must have been like to open it up and see a blur, no words, just black dots organized in rows on a paper. What meaning could formulate in anyone's mind after having just lost nine members of their family?

I met with her in the wee hours of the morning, where no one could follow her. Time didn't seem to matter to Elizabeth at this point; she appeared disconnected, her whole world was missing; mother earth had lost her soul.

My only concern was to find out the truth about a mother of nine biological children of her own and several grandchildren that had passed on; who was Elizabeth.

She began to tell me about her family. She discussed the difficulty of her family being so spread out for safety reasons; it was hard for them to meet in person unless it was at a disclosed location at variant times of the day or week so that they would not be followed. Not even her own sons knew where she lived; for fear that they too might bring the media or other unwelcome visitors because of their TV exposure.

"They recognize my daughters' faces; they are all on TV," expressed the heartbroken Elizabeth, sullen with grief and deep vexing emotion.

Her raspy calming high-toned voice was very patient, and cautious, as she calculated each thought and message she wanted to portray. Nevertheless, this was a woman people made a monster out of, a woman people thought should feel ashamed, but a woman rightfully misunderstood through her dark brown-eyed gaze.

The donation she received from us would be for her daughters; a few articles of clothing to get by, with food they would be okay for a while. She explained how they weren't able to get jobs since the case began.

In a two and half hour meeting with Elizabeth, I found out everything she wasn't; a woman had been persecuted by the media, neighbors and others who said they knew her—even her own brothers.

She timidly greeted me with a slight pleasant smile; I offered her some morning tea or fruit, which was politely declined. In her open-toe black heels that lengthened her usual height of 5'1 or so, she delicately walked to the sofa to have a seat. Long, black, curly locks rested on her shoulders, dancing slightly down her back. Her defined part down the middle of her hair lay flat, displaying some loss of follicles due to stress and trauma. An otherwise youthful face displayed painful lines drawn by tears, frowns and other emotions she endured. Her grief stricken body was fighting to hold up under the immense pressure.

The silence filled the air when neither of us could speak or decide what to say. But in the openness of the silence, her voice managed to find words of courage.

"I don't know what you want or what you want me to say," Elizabeth started. "I really appreciate the help." She looked down, tracing her desolate thoughts of despair to find the right words to say without offense.

"My son Serafino told me you guys were nice people and I just wanted to meet you in person…It's hard for me to trust anyone anymore," explained Elizabeth, who went into her horrible experience with a news anchor she knew by name. She explained the hurt and violation she felt after she realized what happened, after the newscast aired—never again would she allow a sit down interview with any of the media, with any of her children.

"Fino is the outspoken one; he just turned 19 in February…there's hatred out there but he doesn't believe it would happen to him," said Elizabeth with a sorrowful worried look over her son. In her heart, she knew the time would come for him, when things would get rough and people would discriminate against him.

In her sincerity and very humble and appreciative tone, I noticed her strong pride that would uphold what was left of the Wesson family values: they prefer to work rather than receiving handouts from people.

Her life turned upside down in an instant, Elizabeth felt it had been completely stopped; it's almost as if she were living in a deep dream that seemed so blissful until she awoke to the horrid nightmare of reality in her own home.

"The only hope I have and care I have is for my daughters; their future, what type of life they will have."

Through her ocean of pain, Elizabeth mentioned that we had been the first to help in the four months they were struggling to make ends meet.

"We are not like the Charles Manson family or anything like that; people portray our family as monsters," responded Elizabeth to the many commentators expressing their similarities to other mass murders or serial killers. "We are human, we are a family; those were my children," said Elizabeth breaking down into an overflow of tears, she continued, "and people don't know, I loved those children too. They really don't know my family. They think they know us and portray us on the TV as monsters."

After the tears dried, we talked about the many other things happening in her transformed life, such as the land in Santa Cruz, which they were leasing and paying $1,000 a month to the owner. Unfortunately after the owner died, the son took over and would not honor their verbal agreement; the property was sold for $500,000— Elizabeth could do nothing because all of her paperwork to prove this would be on the motor home which the police would not allow her to search. An attempt was made to get her clothing, passport and the receipts to prove they were paying on the property in Santa Cruz; the motion was denied

While checking into reasons of why police would not release her stuff or the judge would deny such a motion, criminal attorney Leslie Westmoreland explained that the judge had a right to evidency value: "I do not know the prosecution's theory," said Westmoreland, "I doubt they have had time to go through every piece of evidence." The State has to show that they need her items for evidence. He then explained that Elizabeth may have been too early in her request, but that she still was entitled to go through her items that she needed.

Elizabeth also spoke about her oldest sons who lived in Santa Cruz saying they were being discriminated against and called racial slurs.

Admiring the beauty of the children and their many shades of brown, Elizabeth described how amazing it was to have children from light to dark; remembering her first experience when she moved to San Jose, Ca.

"When I first moved to San Jose when I was six, we only lived around white and Hispanic people. I remember telling my mom, 'Look at the dark people'," she gleamed with slight embarrassment. "I didn't know how to describe them, I was only six! I just saw they were different, that's all. We were very sheltered."

We also went into the media hysteria regarding the coffins and the vampire connection that would have a community filled with fear and disbelief.

"It just so happens, right before this case—I'm into Anne Rice—my husband had these coffins; he's very crafty. We were going to make furniture out of them. And then I watched the media link the coffins to the deaths. They also took my books; no one reads them but me."

Elizabeth then explained the hard work all of her daughters and nieces put into the house on Hammond.

"The girls worked hard with their own money to get that house on Hammond," said Elizabeth very disappointed at the past events. The guy who sold it to us said it could be residential or commercial," she said, pointing out the dishonesty of the realtor.

In refuting the neighbors responses about her family, Elizabeth said she didn't know any of the neighbors on that street, and she felt that they made the stories up: the wearing of veils to cover their faces and all black to hide their skin. Elizabeth said the only time she wears black to cover up is when she goes to court to hide from any media or to seem obsolete to the community. She also wears the color often for the same reason most women do; black is a slimming color that hides the womanly figure the best, especially if she has gained a little weight, explained Elizabeth.

She also refuted the idea of people and family members saying she was submissive and abused by her husband, Marcus—Elizabeth said she felt sorry for any woman who had to go through spousal abuse, considering herself to be a strong woman that would never put up with such behavior from Marcus. Feeling that description did not fit her, she continued on confidently and with ease, demonstrating her distance from such a ridiculous thought.

Going into her visits with her husband at the jail, Elizabeth talked about the lack of privacy to talk about plain ole family business regarding the children or anything else—"They have their noses pressed against the glass, listening to see what we are saying, to see if there is any evidence to use," she said. Elizabeth also explained her interrogation experience where she was unaware of her rights; she gave another statement to the police when she wasn't as distraught, the police said that the statements from the night of the murders and her current one did not match.

With modest pride, Elizabeth jovially talked about the intelligence of her children and how well mannered they are.

"People often ask if we have an accent...they thought Marcus was black Irish," as she giggled, "they expect my children to speak street talk or black slang—all of them were taught to be well-mannered."

Family is an important part of her life. And yet Elizabeth only communicates with her sister Rosemary, out of all of her siblings. Her brother Eddie who spoke against her on a television interview and who stated he was fearful for his life because of the Wesson family, was in prison for seven years, according to Elizabeth, giving the public a false view of her family that he hadn't been around in years. Her other brother Mike who spoke out against the eccentricities of the family was also in and out of jail. Nevertheless, she continues a relationship with her sister Rosemary, who has always had a severe drug problem and has tried to commit suicide twice—that was one of the reasons Elizabeth had always cared for her sister's children, because her sister was unable and is continuing to get psychiatric help.

Fearful of what would happen to her children, Elizabeth again released tears of frustration.

"I'm worried about the future of my children; what will they do now? Now they don't have a future," hopelessly crying for the loss of her daughters' innocence. Her daughters, for whom she had hoped to build a different life; Elizabeth and Marcus had hoped to build a home one day for them and all of their children, build them furniture from the exotic coffin wood. Marcus would handle all of their accounts when they worked, putting their money away so that they would have something in the future—that would be the only reason all of the money the girls worked for would go to him, explained Elizabeth.

This would be the experience that would change our outlook on this case; the public would be aware of our new perspective and our prior revelation where it was apparent the daughters were not accomplices but victims. They just were not in the room to experience what their other siblings and children experienced: the instant loss of life. Had that happened, the intensity of Elizabeth's pain, I'm sure, would have been maddening; comprehension would have never existed where death totally gobbled life. Yet, these young women were still living victims of a lifetime of manipulation, incest and isolation. It would take numerous years, if ever, to ground and re-etch their experiences to any meaning other than that of deep love and understanding for their master, their father, their husband.

With no peace and the lack of his presence being their new reality, will their minds ever become free enough to see life's possibilities as anything other than what they were taught?

Compassion, empathy and a little assistance would be the best help for this family who is still in denial. They have, yet to go through the process of awakening to what really went on all those prior years. The community and the world would need to learn compassion…

What happens next in the case? How will Marcus be charged and what are the chances that he will get the death penalty? With these worries going through Elizabeth's mind, one can only hope that the verdict is a just one, after all evidence has been presented; however, most of the public already sees Marcus as guilty until proven innocent. The final verdict is yet to be revealed.

To put the world right in order, we must first put the nation in order; to put the nation in order, we must first put the family in order; to put the family in order, we must first cultivate our personal life; we must first set our hearts right.

~Confucius

"Be not deceived; God is not mocked: for whatsoever a man soweth, that shall he also reap."

~Galatians 6:7; *The Bible*

Revelation 11

Final Chapter: Questionable Answers to the Marcus Wesson Case

Marcus Wesson entered the jail at approximately 300 pounds and has already dropped over a hundred pounds. He's isolated at the Fresno County Detention Facility where he is keeping physically fit, preparing for the trial or preparing for his sentence…

"It's quiet—he has a quiet demeanor," said correctional officer at the facility, Darlene Burch. "He doesn't speak, he doesn't request things. You know a lot of inmates they fill out request slips every day for pencils, paper, when's my court date, when's this, when's that, change my business. He doesn't do any of that from the time that I've watched him… He gets up, he sits up, he lays down. He'll do maybe 10 or 15 push-ups. And he'll go to the toilet, he'll come back, he'll sit down, he'll lay down."

When people greet him, he simply does a slight wave; Burch was the first person Marcus waved to some eleven months ago.

Marcus is treated with the utmost respect, as with any other inmate.

"You know we just treat them as they're human beings. We don't pass judgment."

Ironically Burch remembers going to the same church as Marcus in San Bernardino, Ca. when she was a little girl; she didn't know him that well but her three uncles who now live in Atlanta, Ga. knew him.

Although in isolation, Marcus is watched 24 hours a day to assure that he does not harm himself or commit suicide, possibly using his own hair, before the trial begins.

"Because of the charges against him, yes, he definitely has to be under protective custody and he's under watch because of fear he might commit suicide," explained Burch.

Perhaps Marcus is preparing for the gritty trial that will soon begin; many revealing facts will spill into the community, skewing the public's viewpoint. Can this be avoided? Good question!

The jury pool has been overwhelming for the Fresno community; every juror seems to have an opinion, automatically making Marcus Wesson guilty before proven innocent. The process is so arduous because the case is high profile and people are already set in their ways, according to criminal defense Attorney Ernest Kinney. The process takes time...

"Well, most death cases are well-known cases and so the first thing that has to be done is if it's a death penalty case, you have to get a large pool of jurors because two things are going to happen; #1 You're going to lose about half your jurors 'cause the case is so long, they take months. #2 Once, you get that done you have a problem, that you have to death-qualify the jury. Can they give the death penalty. That gets rid of about a third of the jurors. So out of 500 jurors, you're going to lose 300-350 right there. Then, because it's a high profile case, some people may come in and say you know what I've seen pictures of the man, he scares me. I don't think I can be fair, I've dreamt of him. They're gone. So the high profile case is a problem, but the bigger problem is the length of the trial, and the death. That's what gets rid of all your jurors."

Human bias is interfering again; a change of venue has ironically been denied and yet argued by Public Defender Pete Jones who has felt from the very beginning that his client would not get a fair trial. So the selection continues through a tiresome process of choosing the most qualified community members that will be selected to deliberate on a jury that can judge freely without a conscience—going by facts and evidence only. Will they find this unbiased jury?

"It's very difficult not to be biased, but in the court of law, we have to put bias to the side," explained Dr. Hickey:

The jury may have a little bias—we have to be professionals and look at what are the facts, what will carry in court versus our personal opinions, our personal feelings. I may not like what he did—I don't like what he did at all. But I also believe he deserves a fair trial. I believe I could be on a jury even though the situation was horrific. I could hear all of the evidence, and if I could believe—wait a minute, there is reasonable doubt, then that would affect the outcome of the trial, for me. Because I want to make sure that I'm judging by the evidence of the court, not just what I saw on TV, because that's very public opinion—he deserves that, this is our system. Will he get it? There's a lot of evidence against him, not just facts, his whole demeanor, his whole culprit of existence the way he lived his life. Nothing's going to help him at all. So, how do you defend the guy, it's very difficult, who do you blame. It will be tough. If he pleads insanity, I don't think that's going to fly, we'll see.

Pete Jones continues till this day, hoping for a change of venue while the particulars of this case continue to float through the media, drawing in more people who haven't heard about the case but will soon know all. Dr. Hickey, feeling that the venue shouldn't be changed, said that if such a case is done anywhere in the United States, there will be public sentiments, no matter where. For the most part, the Wesson family wasn't even known until the actual murders so it wouldn't make a difference.

Marcus has been requesting a speedy trial from the very beginning of the accusations and although he pleaded not guilty to the charges of the nine deaths; this could have been his way of hiding the family secrets of incest, strong regrets and the religious rite of the Wesson family.

According to Dr. Hickey, in looking at the key evidence that will determine this case, he said it isn't just one piece of evidence, there are a number of factors that will lead to the final outcome:

It all depends on if he wants to take the stand or not in his own defense. The key evidence to look at is residue, blood splats (on the wall), types of murder weapon or weapons, whether there were signs of struggle, premeditation, residue on her: did she (Sebhrenah) fire the gun or did she commit suicide, or did she kill all of the kids and he killed her. They got to sort that all out. There is going to be a lot of forensics evidence they have to solve. They have to take a look at the photographs; they have to look at the prints, forensics evidence, experts testifying to substantiate who did the killing, weapons that were used. They're also going to try to nail if he was the mastermind, (They have to prove that he did it himself, they are going to have to layout and come to a conclusion of how it took place.) Now the coffins; they may have been there because he knew that he's going to do it. Or…someday they were all going to die together. They are going to pull out all of those unusual things, sure that's going to affect the jury—crime evidence they're going to see. They're going to go back into his history and review all this case about this man who was a David Koresh kind of guy and just decided to take them all out.

Predictions of the outcome of this case are very similar; Dr. Hickey, Attorney Ernest Kinney. They both look at the possible influence of Marcus that skews past the evidence in this case. "Either way he is still guilty of mass murder," continued Dr. Hickey, "if he inspired for her to do it, highly unlikely that she would ever do it on her own thinking. She's not going to take away his children because of permission for her to do it herself, because he told her to. So he either did it himself or he told her to do it. Either way it is certainly an unusual case. The minimum sentence he would get for this would be life, no parole. This is the United States, I know that we tend to be easy sometimes on criminals and sometimes on murders, but this is the mass murder of children. I would expect that he would get the death sentence."

Kinney, feeling that the prosecution will stick to going after Marcus and not the daughters or wives as accomplices said it depends on their role; if he aided and abetted the murders then they would be accessories to the crimes committed. They would have to have a strong theory and great evidence to back up those claims. Kinney still feels that the most important evidence of this case would be who the shooter was.

In looking at the defense's take on this case, Kinney said for jury purposes, he would request that his client cut his hair.

"I would have had him cut his hair; I would have had him dress differently because appearances do make a difference. They say in the law, that justice is blind. Well, that's for the judge, but jurors are not blind. Jurors coming into a courtroom saying, you're a Black man, you're not threatening. You look very pleasant. You see Marcus Wesson, and you see those locks, and you see that hair, and you see that size and it's intimidating. So the first thing I would do would be to have him take care of his self better because jurors do draw a lot of inferences just from your looks."

The defense could also use the standpoint of time of death if they want to prove that Marcus couldn't have been in the room at all when the shootings were happening. This could work for or against him. It could be crucial to the final judgment of this case, as Dr. Hickey explains:

"They can determine the approximate time of death. They all died approximately at the same time. Or did they die at different times? So if they died at different times you could argue that they may have died at different locations by how the blood settles in the body, if there is a lot of physical evidence no where, if there's rigor setting or not—they know that rigor sets in a certain amount of time after death, how much the blood has settled in the body, by temperature—if the body's cold versus warm. My mom died, in an hour-and-a-half later she was ice."

Dr. Hickey said the prosecution will come in with loaded guns to win this case: "They'll look at the forensics evidence and the time line, they will bring in experts to talk about the psychological mind control, cult experts, they're going to show a pattern of behavior, how he orchestrated it to happen—I may be wrong because I'm not involved in this case."

Yet, there could be other founding evidence against Marcus or other family members. For instance the practice of taking religion beyond its means or the relation of the Ann Rice books the prosecution could be trying to use as evidence; then something as petty as the names of the deceased victims and other members of the family could be elements to the case. As the prosecution tries to relate the main mother Elizabeth through these books; they might be looking at justified reasons: the time period focused on in most of Anne Rice's books are Old England and the Middle Ages. It could justify some of the names of the victims. For instance, one-year old victim Jeva St. Laurent; the "St. Laurent" is a French name, also a popular given name in the Middle Ages, as a surname it is attested from 1141, according to Ernest Weekely's book *An Etymological Dictionary of Modern English.*

Then there was Marshey St. Christopher whose name means "Christ-bearing." In medieval legend he was a giant (one of the rare virtuous ones) who aided travellers by carrying them across a river. Medallions with his image worn by travellers are known from the Middle Ages. According *toThe Columbia Encyclopedia,* Sixth Edition, his characteristic legend is that one day when he was carrying a little child over a river, he felt the child's weight almost too great to bear. The child was Jesus, carrying the world in his hands. Hence St. Christopher is usually represented as a giant, with the Holy Child on his shoulder; he leans on a staff. He is the patron of travelers, hence the practice of wearing his medal on journeys.

His name was dropped from the liturgical calendar in 1969.

The prosecution may try to surmise with this accomplice theory that the mother was taking erotic images and practices from the book to inflict on her children, as psychologist Carmella explained in regard to impressions on the mind.

However, it can also be noted that Elizabeth was victimized herself, married at 15 years old, knowing Marcus before that, in her impressionable youth, when he harnessed a relationship with her mother Rosemary Maytorena Solorio. This would be a hard point for the prosecution to prove; therefore, they should probably stick to the main accused, Marcus Wesson, as they have threatened before to go after other Wesson family members who were there that day in the house, when the murders took place.

January 24, 2005, each member of the Wesson family was handed court orders barring them from talking about the case. Kinney said the family doesn't have to take the stand, "If they show up and testify, prosecution is okay if they should say something different, they can impeach it but if they say I don't want to testify they've got a problem." (All of our interviews and conversations with any of the family members took place months before this date.)

Again the prosecutors are attempting to use the families' testimony to prove Wesson killed the nine children and sexually assaulted several of the female family members for years—preliminary testimony has already attested to this.

Wesson's former attorney, David Mugridge, said if the family chooses not to testify, it could delay the case, "The court can order them to testify upon threat of ordering them to jail if they refuse to testify, unless they can somehow argue that they are criminally in jeopardy by answering a question, and so call, claim the 5th and then an attorney would have to be appointed."

Another possible piece of key evidence to the sanity of Marcus would be the book he had hand written and sent to Vanity Publishing in New York City. The name of his book is listed in a letter he wrote from jail to *The Fresno Bee* journalist Matt Leedy, *In the Night of the Light for the Dark:*

Hello Mr. Leedly:

I was not writing you off. I am strongly advised not to say anything concerning my case. I have taken it a little further; not to say anything at all to any one. I recieved this letter March 13, 2004. I did however, recieved of your three previous letters.

The men and women at the Fresno Police dept and the Sheriffs dept are professionals and treat me in a consistant manner. In case you are interested: I did write a book about my life and understandings before this mellenium and time period. I sent my manuscript to "Vantage Press"; My handwritten Manuscript, copy of the printed book and a CD are all in the yellow school bus that was confiscated by the Police dept. If you are interested, you have permission to

OVER

follow up on it. There is also a receipt from the Main Post office here on Fresno I had mailed it from. I mailed it December 21, 2002 I believe (about a year a three months ago. The book is titled: " IN THE NIGHT, OF THE LIGHT, FOR THE DARK" I gave this information to a: ▮▮▮▮▮▮ of the Police Department - Multi agency Gang enforcement ~~▮▮▮▮▮~~ Consortium - M.A.G.E.C. Sac Team Supervisor. 559 (▮▮▮▮▮▮ Voice Mail) ▮▮▮▮▮▮ is the phone # ext ▮▮▮▮ . I also gave this info to my two lawyers: Ralph Torres and Peter Jones. Well; that is all that I feel safe to talk about. at this time. I am worried about the safety of my family. Please pray for them.

A friend always,

Marcus Wesson

Could this represent the vulnerable Wesson who's own reality had been broken down, ready to share with the rest of the world his pains? Perhaps this is possible; however, the man is so intelligent, the prosecution feels Marcus doesn't stand a chance to try to plea insanity; if it was premeditated, then he must have known what he was doing. A good question would center on the book that Marcus wrote; it could tell a lot more about his thinking processes and general thoughts about religion and his thoughts on society.

In closing, it is inevitable that Marcus will serve some time at least for the sexual charges, even if he does get the death penalty; death row could take years. Time can only tell as the evidence shouts out the specifics of this bloody murder scene.

The best of prophets of the future is the past.
~Lord Byron (George Gordon Noel Byron)

"And further, by these, my son, be admonished: of making many books there is no end: and much study is a weariness of the flesh."

~Ecclesiastes12:12; *The Bible*

Omega

Where to go now...

Life, at its most precious moment can be understood at the point of death; usually appreciated when it's too late. We'd love to say all the things we could have said and could have done at a desperate moment to stop tragedy before it struck; yet we did nothing. The choices we make in times like this can have a lasting affect, determining where we are today; our conditions are usually a result of our pasts.

What if one didn't have a choice? What if life was all spelled out perfectly for a person, according to someone else's standards? Telling us how to feel, what to expect, our goals, how to live— what if we were living in someone else's world, like the Wesson wives, daughters and sons had done for many years? Unknowingly manipulated by Marcus for so long, the family believed him, and they did not know any better. This is difficult for anyone to overcome by themselves, especially when there are no opposing viewpoints from members of the outside to compare notes.

Judgment is certainly something almost all of us are guilty of in one way or another; we can only base right and wrong on what we know. The Jim Jones, David Koresh and Marcus Wesson cases may not go by our standards, creating the "yuck" factor in the membranes of our minds that cannot comprehend families that allow things like this to happen...

Who are we to say what is normal?

In our own lives there is a certain level of normalcy that simply fades when emotions get involved, depression sets in or trauma plays its role.

Who defines us then?

Somewhere in life, we fall, we come up, we go back down and we come up again: some of us forget to come back up, like Marcus Wesson...life seemed pretty perfect, pretty normal, according to him. Religion kept him and his family out of trouble, it kept him happy, doing the things he loved and with his family. Nevertheless, all was not well, all was not as perfect as it seemed.

Lied to about what's right and what's wrong or abused somewhere in his past, Marcus was not the same Marcus his own mother once knew after spending time in the military service. Our egos block hard-to-deal-with trauma and find a way to cope with it. When it doesn't get dealt with, we suffer the consequences, like Marcus. We suffer the delights of dismay, denial and regret; they weigh on our hearts and souls until we acknowledge the event, the happening, the wrong, the sin. Some of us use religion to judge, to cope, and to live; nothing to an extreme is ever healthy. To an extreme, Marcus so badly wanted to cope with his past, his present and find a way to deal with his future. Hoping that a speedy trial would hide the sins under the rug only back fired because he was reaping what he sowed. Mentally gone and yet looked at as sane, Marcus had clearly defined his right and wrong; living in a society that was very wrong during Jim Crow, discrimination and other racial profiling incidents. No, that wasn't fair, and it wasn't right; those moments in our history are to teach us that we are also human with imperfections waiting to be corrected by some great leader. Marcus felt he was that great leader to correct all of the wrongs in a society that was unfair to him; he would not let these tragedies happen to his family, the things he went through would not be experienced by the ones he so dearly loved. Therefore, he would become that leader of change, knowledge, godliness; keeping his family less than one foot away, controlling how society would tamper his family's belief system, faith, and morals. Society can be cruel, but the mind can be much crueler.

Never in a million years did I ever think I would be writing a murder mystery novel that involved my setting, affect my students I teach, or my own psyche of understanding. I learned compassion in this overly long analysis, no matter the circumstance; the true meaning of victim, and the idea of detachment from judgments that should, but no longer affect me.

I certainly learned from the Wesson family that there are very different families that hold values to the highest degree, obedience to its highest level and religion so pure it becomes tainted. Religion is a set of beliefs that can change anyone from good to bad and from bad to very good.

I still remember using my grandmother as an example; I was quite fearful that the devil was under the ground and was going to come and take my soul whenever I acted out of line or disobeyed my parents. This was a belief instilled in me as a child, creating the desired affect of obedience. Not knowing anything else, I followed until I got older and felt otherwise—compared outside notes.

The more and more I studied this case, the more I was able to understand things about myself, people in my family and the actions of others; unfortunately, the Wessons were judged for actions that happen in families everyday. The difference for them? Murder.

Luckily there is a present and a future that allows healing to take place as time passes by, taking a little bit of pain away each day. A community can heal from this by caring, taking notice of things that may seem out of the ordinary and confronting it; whether it be through the authorities or the individuals involved. Judging someone based on their wrongs does not stop the problem, it only conflicts the situation much more, making the parties in question defensive and feeling misunderstood. We must embraces the knowledge we learn from others, which we can use to help ourselves, our own families and our communities. "It takes a village to raise a child, a community to raise a nation."

How will children know the difference between what is right and what is wrong, if they are never taught?

The seed starts in the womb, and then it is nurtured by its parents; we can either selfishly create a society of ignorant misfits or an empathetic society of curious children bringing knowledge, compassion and enlightenment to the frontier of our existence, our future.

Knowledge is power.
~Aristotle

About the Author

A native of San Jose, Ca., Julia Dudley Najieb resides in Fresno as a writer, high school English teacher and track & field coach.

Since receiving her bachelor's degree in journalism and minor in French from CSU, Fresno in 1995, Najieb has presented and written various pieces of poetry, fiction and non-fiction such as: "The Origins of Racial Epithets," an award winning research thesis presented at UC Berkeley, Claremont Graduate School and CSU, Fresno as a Mc Nair Scholar; "It's the Weekend Special," short story presented at CSU, Fresno short story seminar and "A Little Bit of Spice" romance guide presented in Los Angeles and New York educational seminars as a guest speaker. Her play, *Bench Memoirs*, along with the original 17-minute poetic piece *A Black Woman's Cry for Peace*, both premiered in New York City's Off-Broadway theatres in 2000. *Bench Memoirs* was also presented in a theatrical reading at CSU, Fresno in 2001. Najieb was also the producer and writer of the full-length play *A Black Woman's Cry for Peace* which went on a 10-city California tour and has recently been remodeled to a full length musical, poetic play, to tour internationally under the new name in 2006: *A Woman's Cry for Peace.*

Najieb was also the writer, co-director and producer of the short film, *Reparation Lost*, originally taken from a scene out of her two-hour screenplay, *Stars too High*. The short film was entered into several film festivals and also premiered for the public Feb. 20, 2004 at CSU, Fresno with a panel discussion on the controversy of slavery reparations that followed. The film also aired on a cable station, Comcast Channel 14 with distinguished panelists and live audience questions, hosted by Dr. Arthur Wint of CSU, Fresno. Again the topics were concerning the debate of reparations.

Her company, Ann Marie Production, was developed in honor of her deceased mother, Ann Marie Fowlks Dudley, who died of cancer in 1995. Najieb started off as a sole proprietorship, soon developing a business relationship with her friend Ms. Diva whom she met early on through one of her productions. Ann Marie Production switched over to a powerful alliance of two powerful women in 2004 who now are general partners in the company

On her past time, Najieb enjoys her hobby, dancing, and has been in numerous modern, African and jazz dance performances throughout California. She is also an activist in the community, is involved in various community organizations: Valley Alliance of African-American Educators (VAAASE), Dr. Rev. Martin Luther King, Jr. Unity Committee of Fresno, Elementary Youth Services, Inc., Fresno High School Stomp Team Advisor and Black Student Union Advisor, Fresno Community Kwanzaa coordinator and volunteer, advisor of the "Young Men, Proud Men," just to name a few. Dudley has received various awards such as the Rosa Parks Award for Excellence, the NAACP Award for Excellence as an Activist, National Journalism Award for Excellence, the VAAASE Scholars Award and many others. Najieb is also a member of the Black Chamber of Commerce of Fresno, CA.

REFERENCES

Arax, Mark. "Family Tries to Fathom Killings in Fresno." *Los Angeles Times* 19 Mar. 2004. 15 Aug. 2004 <http://www.latimes.com>.

Ausar, Anuk. <u>Metu Neter Vol. 2</u>. New York: Ra Un Nefer Amen, 1994.

Bach, Marcus. <u>Strange Sects and Curious Cults</u>. 1993: Barnes & Noble Books, 1993.

Bailey, Brandon. "Rigid way of life suggests he is 'charismatic psychopath'." *The Mercury News* 18 Mar. 2004. 30 Oct. 2004 <http://religionnewsblog.com>.

Binion, Dr. Rev. Paul. Personal interview. 6 Jan. 2005.

Burch, Darling. Personal interview. 20 Jan. 2005.

Campbell, NeAisha. "Our Voices." *Naturally NeAisha Enterprises_* . 1 Jan. 2005. Naturally NeAisha Enterprises. 30 Jan. 2005 <http://www.naani.com>.

Charlton, David. "Soldier Who Saves Lives." *First Team Magazine* Summer 1970. 22 Dec. 2004 <http://www.skytroopers.org/medic.htm >.

Dicara, Knotty Vic. "The History Of Dreadlocks." *Knotty Boy*. 2002. Vitamin A Industries, Inc. 9 Feb. 2005 <http://www.knottyboy.com/history.htm>.

Doyle, Jeffrey Scott. "Gun Residue." *FirearmsID.com_*. 2003.

    FirearmsID. 22 Jan. 2005 <http://www.FirearmsID.com >.

Fontana, Cyndee. "The Many Portraits of Marcus Wesson." *Fresno*

    Bee 18 Apr. 2004, late ed.: A1+.

Garcia, Alex. Phone interview. 22 Jan. 2005.

Hickey, Dr. Eric W. Personal interview. 18 Jan. 2005.

    Serial Murderers and Their Victims . Belmont: Thomson

    Wadsworth , 2006.

The Holy Bible. New York: American Bible Society, 1999.

Johnson, Carmella. E-mail interview. 7 Jan. 2005.

Kinney, Attorney Ernest. Personal interview. 26 Jan. 2005.

M., Connie. "In Regards to Marcus Wesson." E-mail to Julia Dudley.

    27 May 2004.

    Phone interview. 27 Dec. 2004.

Morris, Steve. Phone interview. 23 Jan. 2005.

Naba, Bouneith Inejnema. "The History of Dreadlocks." *The*

    *Rising Firefly Magazine_* Sept. 2003. 2 Jan. 2005 <http://

    theearthcenter.com/ff47benben2.html>.

"The People of the State of California VS Marcus Delon Wesson."

    Preliminary Examination, Reporter's Transcript April 8, 2004.

"The People of the State of California VS Marcus Delon Wesson." Preliminary Examination, Reporter's Transcript. April 12, 2004.

Robert, Long Emmet. "Religious Cults in America." The Reference Shelf Volume 66 Number 4. 1994.

Robinson, B.A. "Branch Davidians history, beliefs, and practices." *Religious Tolerance.org.* 19 Apr. 2003. Ontario Consultants on Religious Tolerance. 9 Feb. 2005 <http://www.religioustolerance.org/dc_branc1.htm>.

"St. Christopher." The Columbia Encyclopedia. 6th ed. 2001-04.

Theory, Mad. "Dreadlocks: More Than Just Fashion." *African By Nature Products*. 2003. African By Nature Products. 9 Feb. 2005 <http://www.africanbynature.com/copy.html>.

Weekley, Ernest. An Etymological Dictionary of Modern English. USA: Dover Publications, 1967.